Attitude DETERMINES Destiny

Experience a Better Day Every Day

Bruce Raine

Copyright © 2011 Arbutus TLC, Inc.

Published by Arbutus TLC, Inc.
1004 Commercial Ave # 1095
Anacortes, WA 98221

Printed in the United States of America

Library of Congress Cataloging-in-Publication Data
Raine, Bruce, 1949-
Attitude Determines Destiny / Bruce Raine

ISBN: 1466404175
ISBN-13: 9781466404175

1. Attitude 2. Success 3. Gratitude
I. Title

The use of material from this book for educational purposes is strongly encouraged.

Welcome to *Attitude Determines Destiny*. This book is based upon my life experiences and research from the past thirty years as I followed my path of personal growth.

This is for those who would like to enjoy a richer life. My goal is that this book will be particularly helpful for anyone who is currently dissatisfied with life and wants a life that offers more.

You can improve by reading the book, doing the exercises, and letting yourself grow. Remember that you can also improve your life by paying it forward and helping someone else who could use a hand.

I would love to hear your story. My mailing address is:

Bruce Raine
c/o Arbutus TLC, Inc.
1004 Commercial Avenue # 1095
Anacortes, WA 98221

I am also available for seminars and workshops based on this book's lessons. If you or your group would like to sponsor one, please contact me at www.BruceRaine.com. My mission statement is, "I will teach people how to change their lives dramatically." This goal comes from the struggles of my own life and the desire to help others to have a better life.

Thank you for your time and effort. I hope that this book helps you, and I hope that your experience and your efforts can help others in the future.

Attitude Determines Destiny

Purpose of the Book

You have great potential. We all have treasures hidden inside. They were there before we were born, but they may have been buried under our life experiences. I want to help people discover and develop those treasures within and experience peace and joy and fulfillment in life.

This book is for anyone who wants to get more out of life. Whoever you are and whatever your circumstances, you can make your life wonderful. It doesn't matter what your current circumstances might be, even if you're:

- ☑ Feeling unfulfilled
- ☑ Divorced
- ☑ Widowed
- ☑ Depressed
- ☑ Contemplating suicide
- ☑ Feeling unloved, worthless, insignificant
- ☑ Unemployed
- ☑ Feeling life has no meaning

No one's life should be wasted. God created us to have a wonderful life filled with purpose and meaning. If you don't believe in God, don't let that be a stumbling block. I believe that God loves you just the same. He approved of you before any human being ever showed you disapproval.

What is your purpose? I don't know. Only you can know that. Through prayer, meditation, introspection, and searching, you can find it, even if it takes years. What would be better, to discover those gifts now or to never find them at all?

Purpose doesn't mean that we have to go out and save the world. *Having purpose simply means doing what God designed us to do.* We will know our purpose when we do what truly makes us feel fulfilled and when we use our gifts and talents.

Think about a farmer who for years was poor because he only grew enough to feed himself and a little extra to sell. One day a geologist came by and discovered that the farm was situated on a massive oil deposit. Overnight the man went from poor to rich—or did he? In reality, he was always rich; he just hadn't discovered what he already possessed. Many of us are like that with our gifts and talents. We may not have known what they were or that we had them because we weren't able to discover and develop them.

We have the potential to live a meaningful life. We need to do two things to get there:

1. We must *discover* our gifts and talents
2. We must *develop* our gifts and talents

We are responsible for how we live our lives. Like the farmer, we can live a life of poverty (one without purpose or meaning) or we can live a life of riches (one filled with purpose and meaning). It is up to us. We have the resources we need.

I wrote this book to be a simple guide. I hope that it encourages you to begin your journey of personal growth. I also hope that it helps you fulfill the objectives that you have recognized within but were too afraid to work toward. Life can only get better if we work at personal growth.

Nothing I say or do and nothing I write can ever change your life. Only you can do that. If you act on what is in this book, I believe with all my heart that your life will change for the better.

Thanks

Who I am today is the result of the effort of many people. I want to thank you for your influence in my life.

For help in writing this book, I want to thank Lauren Sampson, Roberto Dorsetti, Alan Johnson, Bruce Rolfe, Terry Slotemaker, Carla Woods, Kathy Baird, Kathy Ewen, and Ron Larson. The time and effort you invested reviewing my draft was truly amazing. I appreciate your feedback and have integrated much of it into this version.

I also want to thank the people at CreateSpace who took my manuscript and made it into the book that you are reading.

Introduction

Attitude is everything!

I'm glad that you've decided to change your life and that this book is part of that process. But if you're like many readers, you may not make it to the end of the book. If you commit yourself to completing this book, then I congratulate you. Your life will change because you'll take the lessons from this book (and others that you read) and develop your own plan for improvement. There is no one perfect plan: read and study different material and then take what works for you from each source to form your own plan.

Change can happen overnight or over a long time. No matter how long it takes, *personal growth can be one of the most powerful forces in life*. Your life will be better for having read this book, especially if you put some of the information into practice.

If we want to make positive changes, we must take action. Some advice will not make sense at first or may not seem to bear fruit for a long time, but if we want change, we will follow it anyway. Consider the following example.

Let's grow flowers from seeds. Here's how we do it:

Human Action Steps

1. We picture in our minds what the flowers will look like.
2. We purchase the seeds.
3. We prepare the soil.
4. We plant the seeds.

5. We water the seeds.
6. We weed the garden.

Steps 1 through 6 give us no immediate feedback

Natural Results

7. Seeds sprout in seven to ten days.
8. Flowers bloom in thirty to forty-five days.
9. Once the flowers bloom, they just keep coming.

Life is similar. If we want a wonderful life, we need good self-discipline. We may need to work for a long time even when we receive no visible results. Then all of a sudden, life will bloom, and it will be wonderful.

To have a successful life, we need to work on it like we do on the garden. We begin by picturing what we want our lives to look like. This can come as a result of prayer or meditation. Then we take the necessary preparatory steps to lay the foundation for our lives: we set goals to achieve our dreams. We practice self-discipline as we strive toward our goals when we receive no immediate positive results. Once we have set a solid foundation for life, we will continue to receive positive results for a long time. The earlier in life we begin this work, the more time we will have to reap the benefits. But it is never too late to begin.

How Do You Spend Your Energy?

I recently had some discussions with a management team dealing with employees with poor attitudes. They described how the employees had put so little energy into what they were supposed to do yet they spent so much energy getting around the rules. The team explained that if these people spent their energy trying to do their jobs as well as they could, they would make the workday a better experience for themselves and for everyone around them.

Introduction

Our attitude affects not only us, but also those around us—our spouse or partner, family members, friends, co-workers, clerks in stores, waitresses, and others. *The good news is that we get to choose our own attitude.* We don't inherit it from our parents and then can never change it. We can choose attitudes for each day and for each situation. We can choose the attitude that will give us the greatest satisfaction in life. The best one will contribute greater enjoyment to those around us also.

I'm not saying that we should choose a selfish attitude and try to make only ourselves happy. This is short-sighted and leads to a great deal of unhappiness down the road. Instead, we can choose an *Attitude of Gratitude* and be thankful for everything in our lives. Adopting this attitude will eliminate many of the small problems that are encountered daily. Not adopting this attitude means that we will spend a great deal of energy overcoming minor difficulties.

It is a simple choice that we can make every day in every situation.

How to Get the Most Out of This Book

In order to get the most out of this book, experience it, absorb it, and then *take action*. You'll realize the effort has been worthwhile when you see the benefits you can receive. Consider the following:

1. Look at what's not working for you and let that motivate you to apply the information in this book to those problem areas.
2. Read one chapter each day, preferably when you are the most alert and rested. Pick the time of day when you're at your best.
3. Read each chapter slowly and underline the parts that are significant to you. Reread a chapter before going on if you need to fully understand it.
4. Get a notebook and do the exercises diligently. You'll find the greatest opportunities for change in them.

5. Each day, use one of the points from the book.
6. Reread the book every month until you feel that you have a good understanding of the material. Then reread it once a year because as you grow, you'll get something different from the material each time.
7. Keep a journal of how you applied this material and what its effects were. It's amazing how life changes when you become aware. Journaling is one of the best ways to become aware of what you're experiencing.
8. This book is only a beginning. Hopefully you'll continue to grow by reading other books and taking other actions to improve your life. Personal growth should be a life-long process.

Use of the Word Happy

In this book, when I refer to "happy" or "happiness," I mean long term inner peace and contentment. I'm not talking about a momentary feeling of excitement based on current circumstances. The main difference is the time involved. True happiness should last longer than a momentary response to favorable events.

Use of the Word Success

When I use the word "success" or "successful", I do not refer to material success or fame in today's world. I define success as achieving what we were designed to do. We all have unique gifts and talents and to discover what they are and then to be using them is true success.

Contents

Thanks ix

Introduction xi

How Do You Spend Your Energy? xii

How to Get the Most Out of This Book xiii

Chapter 1: Why Change? 1

Chapter 2: Goal Setting 13

Chapter 3: Body-Mind-Spirit Triangle 29

Chapter 4: Body = Health and Energy 41

Chapter 5: Mind = Knowledge, Discipline, and Wisdom 51

Chapter 6: Spirit = Belief, Faith, Confidence, and Inspiration 63

Chapter 7: Rocks to Diamonds Cycle 73

Chapter 8: Rocks = Our Potential 79

Chapter 9: Effort = Using Our Potential 89

Chapter 10: Result = Benefit of Our Effort 103

Chapter 11: Belief = Changed by Result 113

Chapter 12: Yes We Can! 125

Chapter 13: Let's Go! 137

Appendix A: The Three Pillars of a Successful Life 141

Appendix B: The Only Laws We Need 143

Appendix C: 100% Money Back GUARANTEE!........... 145

About the Author 147

Chapter 1: Why Change?

Know Thyself
Plato

When Do You Live?

We don't know when we're going to die, and we don't get to decide how it will happen.

Unfortunately, we are dying from the day we are born. The question to ask isn't "When are we going to die?" but "How are we going to live before we die?" Remember the saying, "We are not alive if we are not living."

Too many people die with their music still in them. In other words, they fail to live life to the fullest. Whatever we believe about what happens after death, we must live intentionally here on Earth.

To do that, *we must live in the present.* Too many of us live in the past or the future and then miss out on the present. We lose out on today. If we aren't doing something today because of what happened to us in the past or something we inherited at birth, then we are living in the past and not the present. Just because something was true in the past and limited us in some way doesn't mean that it has to limit us today.

Let's say that you had a bad childhood and find that it limits you today. Why would that be? For example, if your father beat you when you were nine years old, what has that got to do with today? We must learn to leave the past behind because its history and we can't do anything about it. *We only have the power to change the present.* You can't change the beating you received or the feelings you felt then, but you can change the way it affects you today.

Likewise, we can't live in the future, giving up today for tomorrow. When we do, we lose today. Some people who are unhappy today feel that they will be happy when an event happens in the future. For example, consider marriage. Frank who is single is unhappy because he's single. He laments that he'll be happy only when he's married. Years later, he marries Becky, but he's still unhappy and laments that he'll only be happy when he gets divorced. People who think like this never live in the present, only in the future. They give away today for the belief that they will be happy later. Generally, these people will always be unhappy in their current circumstances, no matter what they may be.

As so often is the case, some people are unhappy because their happiness depends on something outside of themselves, on other people or events. We need to learn how to be happy *now*, no matter what we're doing or what's going on in our lives. If we're unhappy, *we* can take steps to make ourselves happy. The quickest and easiest way is to think of what we're grateful for. No matter what our circumstances, we can always be thankful for something.

Escape Your Past

I wasted many years of my life because I lived in the past. I always felt cheated because my family and my childhood weren't happy and fun. How naïve I was to think that everyone had happy childhoods except me! It took years of counseling to get over my past and to start living in the present.

I had a giant "AHA" moment one day during counseling. After a few years of hard work to overcome dwelling on the past, I had an experience that indicated a huge change had occurred.

I always felt that I had this large hole in my soul that was preventing me from feeling successful. One day as I was meditating, I physically felt a movement inside, and I felt this hole close. I learned that that hole was the pain of my childhood. It was the center of my life until that day.

Up to that point, my therapy focused on my past and my problems in childhood. After that day, my therapy and thinking focused on living in the present and planning the future. The problems that had controlled my life were now nothing more than unhappy memories.

We can overcome our childhoods. For some of us it takes years, but that's better than living in the past for our whole lives.

How do we overcome our childhoods? As you progress through this book, you'll learn how to live in the present moment. To truly enjoy life, we must live in the present and not the past or the future. We can't change the past, and we have no idea what the future holds, but in the present, we have power to make choices and be the person we want to be.

Personal Growth Exercise:

Here is a simple but powerful exercise that will help you overcome past hurts. Before moving on, take time to come up with some specific hurts you've experienced. Hold those in your mind as you work through the exercise.

Positive affirmations are a repetition of positive statements that assist us to change our beliefs. This exercise addresses the source of the old beliefs and uses positive affirmations to create new beliefs that will be more beneficial.

On a piece of paper, draw a line down the middle to make two columns. At the top of the left column, write, "God Made Me." At the top of the right column, write, "My Parents Taught Me." Use the space below each heading to write down what your parents taught you and then write how God made you. Here is what I used—it changed my beliefs about myself in a short time:

God Made Me	My Parents Taught Me
God made me loveable	You are unworthy There is something wrong with you You are not loveable
God made me powerful	You are weak You have no gumption You are not perfect
God made me happy	You can't be happy
God made me filled with Peace and Joy	You are depressed You should commit suicide

Every day, in the morning and evening, read the left column aloud to make this external affirmation an internal belief. This is a quick and powerful way to make changes. Some problems will take more effort to resolve than others, but this is a good first step.

Stop and complete this written exercise before going on!

Be part of the successful 2 percent and complete the exercise now!

I believe that only 2% of the people who read a motivational book actually do the suggested exercises and therefore get the most from the book. Please be part of that 2% and diligently do the exercises as you progress through the book.

Where Do You Live?

Do you say or think things like this:

> I hate getting up in the cold or dark!
> I can't stand (fill in the blank)!
> I hate my neighbor!
> I hate my job!

If we live too much in the outside world and have not developed a sense of self, our circumstances will dictate our moods and how we experience each day. We will live only in a reactionary state, where we react to our circumstances without really thinking rationally first. Our experience of life will be negative.

However, if we have developed a sense of self, the outside world will influence us less. If we have a strong sense of who we are and what we are doing in the world, we will dictate our moods and how we experience life. We will live proactively and decide how we want to experience each day.

For example, I live in Anacortes, Washington, which is north of Seattle. Many Californians who move here complain about the winters because the days are short and sometimes lack sunshine (some people would consider this an understatement). But people who grew up here don't let the gray skies get them down: they put on their raincoats and go about their normal business

We have to choose our behaviors each day and not simply react to the circumstances in which we find ourselves.

I find this method to be helpful. Before I go to bed at night I make a written list of five to ten goals I would like to accomplish the following day. When I get up each morning, I have specific things that I want to do. I try not to let the outside world affect my plan. I dedicate my first hour or two each day to physical exercise and my daily Bible devotions. This is a great start to the day!

Depending on what I have planned for the rest of the day, I either get ready to go or I continue reading, turning to other motivational material.

I try to start every day like this. It doesn't matter what is going on around me during this period because I'm living in my inner world. It is a time to connect with inner peace and contentment.

Many people say that they never could do that. That's a choice, and *the way we experience life is a result of the choices we make*. I choose to start my day like this because it engages my body and gets it ready for the day's activity. It also engages my mind because I exercise it when it's most alert. Finally, it engages my Spirit and raises my experience of life to a higher level. I challenge you to try this routine for a month and see how your life changes for the better.

Like many people, I love the long sunny days of summer. But I try to not allow the sun or rain or light or dark to determine how I experience my life. If we in the Northwest allowed rain to prevent us from doings things, we wouldn't get much done.

Motion Leads to Emotion

What do you need to do to be fully alive? I don't know. Only you can know what your purpose is. However, I hope that I can help you discover your purpose. The good news is that we have everything inside ourselves today that we will need to live a full life. We only need to *discover* what we need and then *develop* it.

Purpose is like a muscle. We need to exercise it to fully develop it. Just like a muscle, our purpose will respond to the amount of activity we engage in and grow accordingly. The meaning in our lives will depend on our ability to *discover* our purpose and to *develop* it. We must always look inside to find purpose and meaning in life. Too often our society teaches us to look outside ourselves for meaning. By looking outside ourselves I mean that people turn to food, alcohol, drugs, sex, or other crutches to get meaning. They don't work!

I want to encourage you to live life on purpose, with a purpose. The Greek philosopher Socrates said, "*The unexamined life is not worth living.*" I would say instead, "*The unexamined life was not really lived.*" This is true if we exist through life but take no positive action to make it good. We are given a limited time on Earth, it may be five years or seventy-five years or one hundred and five years, we can't know. No matter how long, life is a gift from God, and it is wonderful. We can waste it or have a rich meaningful life. We must decide to live life to the fullest to be happy.

Do you approach life in a passive, reactive way? Do you approach life in a positive or proactive way? Do you think about your life, what it means, and what you want to do with it?

Do you live each day as it comes with little thought about what you want to do? Do you find yourself tired, bored, and unmotivated? These are all signs of an unfulfilled life.

Guess what: it's your life; you can do almost anything that you want with it. If you feel lethargic, you can change that with some physical exercise. If you're bored, you can change that with some mental exercise. If you're unmotivated, you can change that with some Spiritual exercise.

Well, I just described the whole book in one paragraph. I hope that you don't stop reading. I would like to present to you a *simple* plan that anyone (and I mean absolutely anyone) can use to change their life from something less than dynamic to a life that is full of energy, meaning, purpose, fulfillment, and personal satisfaction.

Too often we want to take shortcuts in life. For example, we may set as a goal "to be happy." We tend to believe that happiness is some magic state that we can reach and live in without doing anything. So how do we try to get there? Drugs, alcohol, sex, love, work, money, you name it. But what happens? Do these factors give us lasting happiness? No, they give us only short-term pleasure followed by a period of greater unhappiness than we started with. Life becomes like a roller coaster. The higher the highs, the more excited and happy we are. However, these highs don't last and are followed by lows, so we feel worse. The lows drive us to seek higher highs. This pattern leads to destruction and despair, not lasting happiness. I believe that this is how many addictions begin.

Think of this amazing paradox: if we seek a shortcut to freedom, we will become a slave to that shortcut. But if we take the right route, we will be truly free. For example, when Fred was a teenager, he always studied and worked hard at various odd jobs. His friends were always out playing and drinking and doing drugs. At the time he envied them because they were having fun and seemed happy while Fred was stuck working and studying. However, many of his friends ended up addicted to drugs and alcohol, but Fred continued on to college and a good career. Therefore, their shortcuts to freedom led them into the bondage of addiction, but his sacrifice led him to a life of freedom.

Real lasting happiness comes not from instant gratification; it comes from doing what we were designed to do. *Remember, you were designed for a particular purpose.* All of us have our own unique purpose. It was inside of us the day we were born. The choices we make in life either lead us closer to that purpose or further away from it. The closer we get to that purpose, the better our lives will be and the more fulfilled we will feel. But to find that purpose in life, we must look inside ourselves, not outside. We must get in touch with our *bodies,* our *minds* and our *Spirits* and listen to what they tell us.

Distractions

Unfortunately, it is very difficult in our present day of instant communications to find the time for introspection. Strangely enough, today's instant communication devices were supposed to save us time and free us up to enjoy our lives. But instead, they often consume our lives. And although we have better communication devices, we have worse communication. For example, let's look at the time we spend in a car:

- ☑ It used to be that a person driving in a car had time to be alone and think about her day or her life. Some people experienced stress in the rest of their day but found that they could relax and have solitude in the car.
- ☑ It used to be that two people driving in a car had uninterrupted time to talk with each other. Traveling together was a time to build relationships with spouses, family, or friends.

- ☑ It used to be that a parent would drive the kids and talk with them. This was valuable time together.

Today in cars, I often see the opposite:

- ☑ When people are driving alone, they are often on the cell phone or doing work instead of relaxing and thinking.
- ☑ When two people are driving in a car, often the driver (not usually the passenger) is talking on the phone. I don't understand this. I often wonder that if the driver is with friend A but talking to friend B. Then later maybe the driver is with friend B but talking to friend A. Why doesn't this person just talk to who he's with?
- ☑ When parents drive their kids, parents often talk on the phone to a friend or do work while the kids in the backseat watch television.

I believe that too often we don't use our modern communication devices in a healthy way. They are meant to serve us and to make our lives better. Too often they seem to rule our lives and steal the quality without us even thinking about it. For example, if the phone rang right now, would you answer it? You are engaged in reading a book that could change your life, yet you might stop to answer the phone. I sometimes hear people answer the phone and say, "I can't talk now. Can I call you back?" Remember that phones have answering machines or voice mail for a reason.

That's enough whining about cell phones. I think they're amazing devices. I just feel that we misuse them like so many other forms of communication. Television, the Internet, computer games, and other forms of entertainment are making us sedentary, solitary people when what we really need is to be more active and involved in relationships.

It only takes a little time and effort each day to make your life come alive. The secret is to take a little time every day for *you* because you deserve it. You really deserve to have a wonderful life.

To illustrate how we can take time to make our lives richer, let's look at a short story by Leo Tolstoy. The title of the story is,

"The Three Questions". Think about how these questions and their answers could change your life.

Question 1: What is the most important time?

Now is the most important time. It is the only time in which we have any power. We do not have power in the past or in the future, but we do have power in the present to make choices.

Question 2: Who is the most important person?

The most important person is the person with us *now*. That person is the most important because he or she is the only one we can interact with.

Question 3: What is the most important thing to do?

The most important thing is to do good for the person we are with *now*. To determine how we can serve that person and to take specific actions to do good is the greatest act of love.

Just think of how this could change our lives. Whatever we are doing, we are focused on the present moment and the person we are with. This will create more meaningful time together and better life experiences. We will have better relationships and will create more good memories of the time we spend together.

Remember the Golden Rule, "*Love Your Neighbor as Yourself.*"

Personal Growth Exercise:

Here is an exercise that I learned from my therapist, Hal Pullin. He recommends that we do this in the morning to focus on what we need each day.

Answer these three questions:

1) What do I feel?
2) What do I want to feel?
3) How can I create what I want to feel?

I strongly recommend that you take a few minutes and answer these questions. The best way I have found of getting the most out of an exercise like this is to write down the answers. When we write the answers on a piece of paper, we also write them in our minds and in our hearts.

Stop and complete this written exercise before going on!

Be part of the successful 2 percent and complete the exercise now!

Summary

One of the greatest lessons that I ever learned is that my attitude will determine how I experience each day and ultimately my whole life. The fact that I get to choose my attitude each day means that I can determine what my life will look like.

Another great lesson was to live in the present. For many years I lived in the past and harbored anger and resentment for what had happened in my childhood. Now that I live in the present I feel free and more powerful.

We can accomplish a great deal by knowing what we want. That can be achieved by deciding in advance what we want, then setting goals to obtain it, and most importantly, taking action to achieve those goals. Let's look at goal setting in the next chapter.

Chapter 2: Goal Setting

The Best Time to Set Goals Was Yesterday, The Second Best Time Is Now

Goals Are the Catalyst of Life

Where are you going?
Where do you want to go?
Many people are unable to answer these questions because they've never thought about them. They get up and go about their lives like they have no choice about what they do. They just float down the river of life and go wherever the current takes them. That will not get us where we want to go, assuming we even know where that is.

Many people don't have goals. This may be hard to believe, but it's true. Many of my students didn't have any goals beyond graduating and getting whatever job they could get right away. In particular few people have written goals. I find that putting my goals in writing is very powerful. It makes a deeper impression on my mind and greatly increases the chance that I will accomplish them.

Would you get in your car and start to drive with no end point in mind? Would a pilot fly a plane with no destination in mind? If so, how would the driver or the pilot know when the trip was complete?

Goals are essential to success. People are often afraid to set goals because they think they won't reach them or that if they don't set goals, they can't fail to achieve them. This is not true. It is better to have a high goal and not quite make it than to have no goal at all. Goals are not permanent; they change as we go through life. It's important to set goals and review them periodically—I recommend doing so at least once a year. Some people review their goals monthly, weekly, or even daily.

When I was a university professor, some of my students would not set goals for fear of setting the wrong ones. They felt their lives might be ruined if they didn't set the right goals. An imperfect goal is better than no goal at all. With a goal, we will get moving forward. We may quickly see that we really want to go in another direction, but goals can easily be adjusted. At least we are on our way. Many students started university with one degree or career in mind but changed during their time at college to a different degree program because they had better information than when they started.

Goals have played a major role in my own success. At age eighteen, my only goal was to leave an unhappy home. Going to college was the solution, but I had no idea of where that would lead me except out of where I was. Later, I got married, had a child, and then got divorced. At that point I thought that my life was pretty much over. But after hearing someone talk about goals, I set a goal to get my MBA at a local college. I never got that degree from that college but eventually got my MBA from another college. However, because I had started thinking of what I wanted and where I wanted to go, my life really got kick-started. Once I started the MBA program, I started to think about other things that I wanted in life.

For example:

Where did I want to live? I discovered that I wanted to live in California and in particular the San Francisco Bay area. I got a job in Hayward, California, and ended up living in the area for twenty-five years.

What did I want to do? I had always felt that my purpose was to teach, so I became a professor and made that my career.

Where did I want to travel? I found that I had many dreams of traveling, and I've since fulfilled many of them. I love Australia and have taken two trips there. I love tropical islands and I've spent many vacations on islands in the Pacific and the Caribbean. Fortunately, there will always be other exciting places to travel.

What kind of hobbies would I like? I realized that I loved to hike, mountain bike, sail, play golf, explore, travel, and more.

Once we set goals and get going, we will just keep expanding our world and our lives.

Let's look at the Corridor Principle, which is really important as we pursue our goals. If we sit at home waiting until the right opportunity comes along, it may never happen or if it does, we may not recognize it. On the other hand, if we set goals and get started, all kinds of opportunities arise that we would never have seen if we weren't taking action to pursue our goals.

This is called the Corridor Principle because setting goals is like a corridor in a large building: when we stand at the end of the corridor, we don't see all the doors down the hall. However, when we start down the corridor we discover that there are many doors of opportunity along the way. If we don't start down the hallway, we will never get to the doors. But as we continue down the hallway, we will discover many doors leading to many wonderful opportunities.

Let's do a little review to see where you are right now. There are no right or wrong answers. This is just an exercise to help you become more aware. You must know where you are at present and where you are going to have a full life.

Personal Growth Exercise:

Assume that you continue to live your life as you are right now. Answer the following three questions:

1. Where do you think you will be in five years?
2. Where do you think you will be in ten years?
3. Where do you think you will be in twenty years?

Action is very important in life. We can't think our way through these exercises. Doing that is like saying that we want to be physically fit, so we're going to think about exercising. It doesn't do any good. Take time to write down the answers to these three questions before you continue reading further. You will learn a valuable skill to use later in the process.

Stop and complete this written exercise before going on!

Be part of the successful 2 percent and complete the exercise now!

Welcome back! How did you do? Are you happy with what you discovered?

For many people, this is an eye-opening exercise. They find it disturbing, but they can't put their finger on why. If you are like many people and go through your day-to-day life without thinking of the long term, then this exercise is meant to get you to think long term. *While we must live in the present, the people who succeed are people who plan for the long term.*

Let's say that we have a long-term goal of becoming a doctor. We must keep this goal in mind when we are doing anything. We must constantly ask ourselves, "Is this taking me toward my goal?" This is long-term thinking guiding our present activities. Becoming a doctor will take years of study, hard work, and sacrifice. We'll have decisions to make every day in the present that will affect that future goal.

We must also think in the short term. To become a doctor, we must take and pass certain courses. If we have the mind-set that this short-term goal is taking us toward our ultimate goal of being a doctor, then it will inspire us to work hard and pass each class.

What if we are not long-term thinkers? Then we'll have much less motivation to pass the class and will have a better chance of dropping out or not doing our best. Long-term goals create energy and excitement that otherwise would be missing from our day-to-day lives. Yes, some people would call this stress, but there are different kinds of stress. Bad stress causes us medical problems and leads us to make bad decisions to escape the stress. However, good stress is a motivator and will propel us toward our goals. The biggest difference is that bad stress is just there and seems to hang around forever. But good stress is there for a time and disappears after we achieve another step toward our long-term goals.

Okay, how are your long-term goals looking? If you think that you don't have any, don't worry about it. We will go through an exercise that will help you determine and set specific long-term goals. There is nothing like a person who is committed to a long-term goal. Goals give us passion and energy. With goals, we will come alive like we have never been before.

Personal Growth Exercise:

Here is a simple exercise I always gave my students on the first day of class. Answer these three simple questions:

1. Where do you *want* to be five years from now?
2. Where do you *want* to be ten years from now?
3. Where do you *want* to be twenty years from now?

This may sound like the same exercise you just did. However, the previous exercise asked you where you *think* you'll be assuming you continue to live as do now. This one asks where you *want* to be. The first exercise showed you where you were headed. This one shows you where you'd like to go in your life.

Stop and complete this written exercise before going on!

Be part of the successful 2 percent and complete the exercise now!

Just think about what you did today. Did it get you closer to the place that you described in the most recent exercise?

This exercise is more difficult than the one before it because it requires us to know where we want to go. To do this, we have to think very carefully about our future and decide what we want to do. As I have said, many people are not aware of what they want. We should not feel bad about not having life goals. I believe that many people were never taught to set goals. It is not part of many educational systems, believe it or not. I hope that the result of doing these exercises is that you are now more aware of what you want to do. It will be necessary to redo these exercises many times in the coming years as you grow and change.

The first set of questions really motivated me. When I first asked myself the question, "Where do I think I will be in ten years?" I was twenty-eight years old. My answer to this question was "dead." Frankly, that didn't appeal to me, so I took action to change my life. Looking back, I truly believe that if I had not taken action, I would have ended up dead, either physically or emotionally, by the age of forty.

Even if you get nothing else out of this book, please set goals for your life. Spend some time dreaming about what you want to do. Pray and ask God what he wants you to do. Look at the gifts and talents that He gave you and think about how best to use them. If you use your gifts and talents and do what you were designed to do, happiness and success will follow.

Do you set New Year's resolutions? I never liked making them because they were usually negative. Many people think, "I am fat. I smoke. I drink. I chew my nails," and they make resolutions to stop those bad habits. But it is very difficult to *not* do something. For example, some of us want to diet, so we spend a lot of energy trying *not* to think about food. But when we are trying to *not* think about food, we think about food. It is better to substitute a new behavior for an old behavior than to try to not do something.

I believe in setting positive goals, such as these: "I weigh 180 pounds on March 31"; "I run fifteen to twenty miles a week by September 30"; "I make five thousand dollars a month by June 30." Then we aim at our goal. If we are positive and precise in stating our goals, we will be more likely to achieve them.

Another important concept is writing our goals on paper. This should be done at least once a year. Brian Tracy, a wonderful motivational teacher, advocates writing out goals monthly or even daily. It never hurts to write them out more often. He states that the power of written goals is much stronger than unwritten goals.

Instead of creating New Year's resolutions, we should spend some time each year reviewing our goals, evaluating how we are progressing, determining if they are still the goals we want, and revising them as we see fit. This will keep us forever going in the direction we want to go. If we never stop to examine our lives and our paths, how will we ever get to where we want to be, or even know what that place looks like?

Elements of a Good Life

Do you know what a good life looks like? Not for me or someone else but for you. What does a good life look like for you? Each of us is different. We must each determine what we want in life in order to find true happiness. Although we might share some ideas with others, our life is and should always be unique. I can't tell you what your life should look like any more than I can tell you what food, clothing, or car you might like or dislike. If anyone ever tries to tell us what we should do in life, we should listen politely and consider what they say but not follow their advice blindly. We must determine what is right for us.

When I was in my last year of high school, I decided to go to university. My teachers and guidance counselors told me that I was wasting my time and would be a "Christmas graduate" (someone who fails out before the first Christmas break). They based their opinions on how I had performed in high school when I was unhappy and had a terrible attitude. However, these were a reflection of my home life that was not very rosy and had nothing to do with my potential or personal desire to succeed.

My only goal in going to college was to leave my unhappy home. I went to college and almost proved them right, but I got by and received my degree in three years. My attitude had not improved a whole lot, but it was getting better. Then in my late twenties, I got divorced, and I was forced to really look at my life for the first time. That is when I really started to take responsibility for my own life.

We must not be discouraged by anything that people say to us or about us. I proved I wasn't a Christmas graduate. My teachers could only see part of me, the exterior part that was heavily influenced by my dysfunctional family. They couldn't see what was inside me, what would drive me to do better than I had done in high school. My teenage years were the worst years of my life, so my teachers saw me at my worst.

What are the elements of a good life? The following are some ideas. We must each determine what is best for ourselves. All the bullet points below are to a large extent interdependent. In other words, we won't be as successful in life if we just have some elements and not the others. We must have a healthy balance.

Primary
- Relationship with God
- Relationship with self
- Relationships with people
- Health

Secondary
- Fulfilling career
- Balanced personal finances

- Satisfying hobbies
- A role in our community

These will change as we go through life. Today health may mean one thing, but in five or ten years, it may mean something different. A relationship with God will mean one thing in our twenties and something different in our fifties. When we are young, we can't conceive of ever being old. Life expectancies are rising all the time, and most of us will live into our seventies and eighties, and some of us will reach our nineties and even over one hundred. The foundation we set today is not just for today. It is for a long time into the future.

We must be sure that we understand what "successful life" means. This does not mean that we become a millionaire or climb Mount Everest. *A successful life means that we achieved what we were designed to do.* Maybe we were meant to be a truck driver and travel the country; then that is a successful life. Maybe we were meant to have a family and raise children; then that is a successful life. For me, it was being a professor, so I feel that I have had a successful life, so far. Success can only be measured by the standard we set for ourselves.

Goal-Setting Strategies

There are many different ways to set goals. We should pick a way that feels comfortable to us and use it. Goal setting is a simple process, but it requires that we know ourselves, which makes it much more complex.

Here are some simple strategies for setting goals:

Strategy 1

Ask our parents, friends, lover, teachers, or others what we should do. This method assumes that these people know us and have our best interest at heart. If we ask an accountant what we should do for a career and he says to become an accountant, it may not be solid advice. This strategy may not provide us with our goals but someone else's, and we can't live our lives for someone else.

Strategy 2

Look at our past and see what we have done before. Determine what we are good at and what we are not good at. Determine what we like to do and what we don't like to do. Have you ever been so absorbed in an activity that the time passed while you were not unaware of anything else? You were in a zone where you were completely content and immersed in what you were doing. We should pay attention to these experiences because they tell us something important about ourselves.

Using our past experiences, we can pick out a course of action to take in the future. Remember, we can change it along the way if necessary. The weakness in this method is that our past may not have given us broad enough experiences to make an informed decision.

However, this strategy may be better than strategy 1 because at least it helps us identify what *we* like or want to do instead of what someone else thinks we should do. Remember that when you set your goals, you are looking for what you were designed to do.

Strategy 3

Brainstorm with some friends. Just throw out ideas with no judgment or evaluation of the idea. Write them all down until we have exhausted our imaginations. Then we can go back and start categorizing them. For example, divide all the ideas into three groups: good ideas, okay ideas, and bad ideas. We'll need to establish some screening criteria to determine what defines each category. The advantage of brainstorming is that we get to consider things that we might not otherwise have even thought about.

Strategy 4

Take a talent inventory or aptitude test. These are tests that show what abilities we possess. There are many free tests on the internet. The test might show us something that we didn't know about ourselves. We may discover a hidden talent.

Strategy 5

Hire a life coach or therapist to help us sort out what it is we were designed to do. This may take some time, but the most important thing is not *when* we figure it out but that we do figure it out before we die. It would be a shame if we lived our whole lives never knowing what it was that we wanted to do. The right coach or therapist can make a world of difference and save us a lot of time. We need to make sure we are confident that our advisor is competent in helping us discover our talents. This is easier said than done.

Strategy 6

Pray and meditate on what it is that we were designed to do. Prayer is asking God for help. Meditating is listening to God for His answer.

Remember that God designed each of us for a special purpose before we were even born. As humans, it is our responsibility to God and to ourselves to find out what that purpose is and then to do it.

We need to be patient if we have trouble figuring out our purpose today. Perhaps we are not ready to know it yet. Perhaps we will find our purpose while we are busy learning who we are. It has taken me thirty years to write this book. It is part of my purpose but I was not ready until now.

If you don't believe in God, then try meditation. This simply means sitting with no distractions and thinking about nothing else. You may also wish to think, "If there was a God, what would He want me to do with my life?"

Strategy 7

I used this strategy after I retired to give my life new direction. I felt a bit lost because I wasn't living with purpose. I had this gnawing feeling that I wasn't doing what God wanted. I've always been good with the process of goal setting, so I didn't really examine the method I was using as I tried to figure out what my new goals should be.

One day I woke up and realized that I was trying to set my goals backwards. I had been starting with what I wanted to do when I should have been starting with the gifts and talents God had given me and how I should use those to serve God and others. Within a day of this change in thinking, I was able to write down a new personal mission statement and long-term goals. Writing this book was a step toward these new goals.

I'm an energetic person, and after this change, I simply took off. My life was full every day. When I had been thinking about what I wanted to do, I was limiting myself. When I thought about my gifts and talents, my goals became obvious. God made me a teacher; there is no question about that, so I thought being a professor was what I was supposed to do. That's why I felt lost after I retired.

But when I thought about what God wanted me to do, I was energized all over. I realized that the years of teaching at the university were not the end goal God wanted for me. It was only part of my training to become the teacher of life skills, God's true intention for me. We will never know true inspiration and passion until we do what we know we were designed for. What could be greater?

Please, before you leave this chapter, do some work to set five-year, ten-year, and twenty-year goals for yourself. Remember that goals are not set in concrete. We should review them at least once a year and see if they need tweaking or a major overhaul.

Personal Growth Exercise:

Write out at least three goals that you are going to achieve during the next:

1) Five years.
2) Ten years.
3) Twenty years.

It doesn't matter if you're eighteen or eighty; this is an important exercise that will energize your life.

Stop and complete this written exercise before going on!

Be part of the successful 2 percent and complete the exercise now!

Make a Dramatic Change in 30 Days

How do you feel about goals and about your personal goals? Did you do the exercises in this chapter? If not, why not?

- I don't want to write them down
- I'll do it later
- I kind of know what I want anyway
- I don't have enough time

Whatever your reason, it is an excuse. Next to belief in God, goal setting is probably one of the most important ways to succeed in life.

Try this 30 Day Challenge and you will make great progress towards your goals. Follow it for thirty days, and I *guarantee* that it will change your life.

1. Write down ten goals you would like to accomplish in the next one to five years. You can use the list from the last exercise if you want.
2. Pick the goal that you believe would make the greatest impact on your life if you were able to achieve it.
3. On a separate piece of paper, write that goal at the top of the page. Below it, write ten things you can do to accomplish that goal.
4. For the next month, spend at least one hour *every* day working toward this goal. Ignore the other goals for the next thirty days and work on this one exclusively.
5. At the end of the month, look at where you are and compare that to where you were at the beginning. I guarantee that if you follow these instructions; your life will change significantly.

This exercise is very powerful because it demonstrates:

- The power of goals
- Our commitment to our goals
- Our self-discipline
- What we can accomplish in just one hour a day

Earl Nightingale, one of the greatest motivational speakers and authors, stated that if we spend one hour a day at something, we will be experts at it in less than three years. If we want to learn a foreign language or to play a musical instrument, this is how to do it.

Did you do the goal-setting exercises? If not, I suggest that you stop reading. Proceeding without doing the exercises will mean that you will get less from the following material. It will be like building the second floor of a building before you've finished the first floor. I recommend that you return to the beginning of the chapter and do the exercises. It is important to write them down as instructed.

Summary

Next to belief in God, setting goals is probably one of the most important ways to succeed in life. People with goals have passion, drive, and focus in their lives. A by-product of living life with specific goals is that we are generally happier people. In addition, others enjoy being around us more.

Success is doing what God designed us to do. Unless we're incredibly lucky and stumble into success, setting goals and working toward them is really the only way to a successful life. People may succeed without goals, but just imagine how much more successful they could be with strong goals.

The 30 Day Challenge is a powerful tool for getting started on accomplishing any goal, whether it is large or small. I use it on a regular basis.

Chapter 3: Body-Mind-Spirit Triangle

The Strongest Shape in Building Is the Triangle

The Three Facets of Our Being

A person's being can be broken down into three distinct parts: the *body*, the *mind*, and the *Spirit*. They are not three separate parts but are interconnected, like a musical triad that must be played together to produce a harmonious sound. We must play the three parts of ourselves like that triad to produce a harmonious life. *When we want to change, we must coordinate the three facets of our being, or we won't be successful.*

Unfortunately, many people don't coordinate the three parts and work on only one. Let's look at a couple of common examples: dieting and quitting smoking. What percentage of people do you think are successful at breaking the two habits of unhealthy eating and smoking? A low percentage!

Mark Twain once said, "*It's easy to quit smoking. I've done it hundreds of times!*" The same is true with dieting: people try over and over.

Why do so many people fail at something that seems so important to them and would seem simple to do? Just stop eating so much. Just stop smoking. It's easy! I believe that the main reason so many people fail is that they fail to coordinate their minds, bodies, and Spirits. As illustrated in the following diagram, all facets are interdependent.

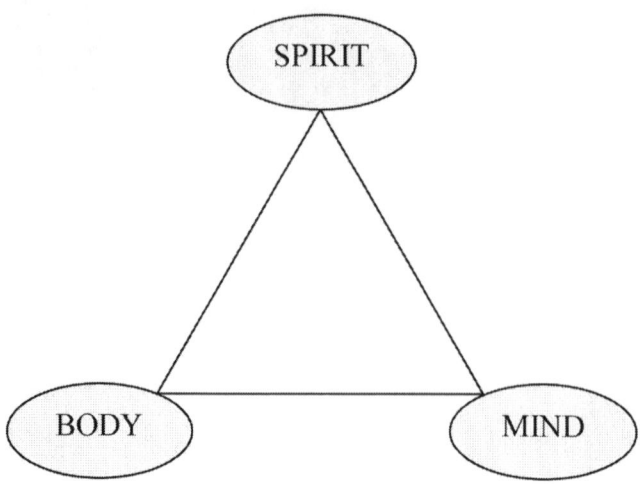

One would think that dieting is primarily a body function. However, if we try to diet without engaging our minds (with knowledge of health and the self-discipline to eat less) and the Spirit (with the belief that the body is a temple of God and the inspiration to be healthy), we will probably fail. The same is true of giving up smoking or just about any other addiction.

Another barrier to changing our behavior is our approach to it. We must approach positively: "I want to be healthy," and not negatively: "I want to stop…" If we believe that we want to be healthy, we have a good chance of success. But if we are only focused on stopping the problem, then we are setting ourselves up for failure. We must focus on what we want and not focus on what we don't want.

If we engage the three elements, we will have fantastic power and a much better chance of success. Let's look again at dieting since it is such a common activity in our country. What does dieting mean to us? Sacrifice? Deprivation? Starvation? For many, dieting is negative and comes with many bad associations. To begin, the word "diet" starts off with the word "die." This is not a good beginning! A better approach to weight management is to set a goal of being healthy. We need to determine a healthy weight range for ourselves and work toward that. A common measurement of healthy weight ranges is the Body Mass Index (BMI), which indicates healthy and unhealthy ranges for our height. The BMI can be found and calculated on the internet.

The first facet (the body) will engage in eating less, eating better quality food, and getting exercise. Our bodies know intuitively what they need for good health. However, with our society's abundance of cheap, unhealthy food and philosophy that food can be eaten almost everywhere and at any time, it is difficult to eat in a healthy manner. If we try to be healthy using our bodies alone, it will be very difficult.

If we also engage the second facet (the mind), we will have a greater chance of success. For example, if we use our minds to research healthy habits and why we should practice them, then we will better understand how to be healthy and that will help us develop stronger self-discipline. Can we resist a rich, gooey chocolate snack? The snack will be easier to resist if we know that it might hurt us than if we feel we should resist simply because we are on a diet.

Finally, if we engage the third facet (the Spirit) and come to believe that God made us to be healthy and created our bodies as temples that hold his Spirit within us, then it will be even easier to do what we need to be healthy. God wants us to be happy. Our good health will bring us peace and joy.

By combining the power of the three facets of our being, we will be better able to accomplish what we want in life. A simple mathematical equation illustrates the power of the three facets. We might expect that the three facets add together. To test this, let's assign each facet a value of 10. The value of our three facets would then add up to 30:

$$\text{Body} + \text{Mind} + \text{Spirit} = \text{Power}$$
$$10 + 10 + 10 = 30$$

But this is not the case! The three facets instead multiply each other's effects, yielding greater power than simple addition. For two facets, the relationship looks like this:

Body x Mind = Power
10 x 10 = 100

These facets generate even more power if we combine them with the third:

Body x Mind x Spirit = Power
10 x 10 x 10 = 1,000

When I try to do something with just one facet of my being, I either don't do as well as I want to or I just don't complete what I want to do. But if I combine a second element, I do much better than I would just using one. If I combine all three elements, then I can do almost anything. I must admit that when I achieve something significant, it is because I combined all three facets of my being.

Sometimes we may feel that we are successful without combining all three elements. I would like to say two things about this assertion: First, are we sure we didn't use more of the elements than we thought? Maybe a good athlete attributes her performance only to physical prowess. But did her mind coordinate and direct that ability to a higher power? Did the Spirit give her the faith to do well? Belief that we will do well is an essential element of performing well. *We can raise our level of performance dramatically if we firmly believe that we will do better.*

Second, if we feel we did well and we truly didn't use all three facets of our being, just think about how much greater we could have performed if we did use all of our being.

Before we leave this discussion of the combination of the facets of life, let's look at another example that shows how the facets combine to result in dramatic power. The facets are not all equal in value. Instead of giving each of the facets a value of 10, I believe that the mind is greater than the body, so it should have a greater value, maybe 100. I further believe that the Spirit is the most powerful of them all and should have an even greater value like 1,000. If we look at the product now, we will see even more power.

Combining the body and mind, we get:

Body x Mind = Power
10 x 100 = 1,000

Combining the body, mind, and Spirit, we get:

Body x Mind x Spirit = Power
10 x 100 x 1,000 = 1,000,000

This explains why some people perform at a level much higher than average. This also illustrates that the Spirit is essential to reaching truly high levels of performance in our lives.

Coordinating the Three Facets

Next let's look at communication, which is such an important part of success. How do we communicate using the three facets of our being?

Body

The body's role is the easiest to understand because we are the most familiar with it and use it so often. We communicate by seeing, listening, and speaking. Two are for input and one is for output. I have heard people say that we are supposed to listen and see more than talk because we have two eyes and two ears but only one mouth—we have four channels to receive communication but only one to send communication.

There is a saying that if you're silent, people might think you're a fool, but if you open your mouth and talk, you will remove any doubt!

Mind

The second form of communication happens with our mind. We are less familiar with this form. Usually we believe that thinking is how we communicate with our minds. That is only a small part of the communication. Our minds have two distinct parts, the conscious mind and the subconscious mind. We must communicate with both parts in order to fully use our minds. In my twenties I learned how to communicate with my subconscious mind. This was a very important discovery. We must understand that the subconscious is there and that it is a significant part of our lives.

I believe that our subconscious mind is where we store information like thoughts and memories over the long term. It is also where we go to retrieve our long-term data. But more significantly, it controls our day-to-day activities like walking, running and driving, without us even knowing it. Our subconscious mind is like a computer that has been programmed to perform certain tasks. It will run those programs over and over without changing them. This can be good or bad. If we have good programs, then we will get good results. If we have bad programs, we will get bad results. The good news is that we can reprogram our subconscious mind, but it takes deliberate effort.

God wrote our original programs for our benefit. However, our parents and caregivers changed them before we reached the age of seven. While we were in the womb and young children, the events that were occurring in our parents' lives were being communicated to us and absorbed by our subconscious. This influenced our views of what the world is like and what we need to do to survive. Many of us don't know what these programs are, but if we ever did something and later wondered why we did it, it was probably coming from our subconscious programming.

For example, when we were learning to drive a car, it seemed difficult and we had to think through each part and concentrate on the task. But now we just drive without giving it much conscious thought. We have moved driving from our conscious mind to our subconscious mind. This is true of anything we do so frequently that it becomes routine. This is how we program or reprogram our minds.

Do you repeat certain ideas to yourself or think recurring thoughts during the day? Many of us do. This is called "self-talk."

Self-talk is nothing more than thoughts our subconscious mind repeats. These messages are communicated to our conscious mind. They can be either positive or negative.

In my world, negative self-talk came from my father. He taught me that I was worthless by constantly repeating what was wrong with me. Therefore, he reprogrammed my subconscious mind with his negative affirmations.

As an adult, my subconscious, which had dutifully stored these messages, constantly repeated them back to me. They were my daily affirmations. My negative self-talk told me that I was bad at sports and would always be a loser. But I had good athletic ability and picked up sports easily. However, I could never win at sports when I was young. When I played tennis, no matter who I played, I always came in second. I have a lot of natural ability for golf, but again I always came in second. I wasn't competitive in sports because of this.

The subconscious mind is powerful and true to its programs and it can control our lives in ways we can't imagine. It's very important that:

- We know what is in our subconscious mind
- We reprogram our subconscious mind to not work against us
- We program our subconscious mind to work for us

As with a computer, we need to know what is in it and to learn to use the programs appropriately. That means learning about our computer. We need to keep the programs that help us and remove ones that don't.

I had to work hard to reprogram my subconscious with positive thoughts. Now my subconscious mind works for me instead of against me. Reprogramming my subconscious is an ongoing job.

What is your subconscious mind doing for your life? In the next exercise, you'll take a few minutes to think about how your subconscious mind is working. Does it send positive or negative messages? Is it helping or hindering you? If you have never thought about a subconscious mind, just take some time to meditate on it and see what comes up.

If you have difficulty with this exercise, try thinking of something that you did that made you think afterward, "Why did I do that? I know better" or "I didn't want to do that."

Personal Growth Exercise:

Write down at least five *negative* messages that your subconscious mind has sent you in your life. Think of situations where you did something and then afterward wondered why you did it and couldn't think of a conscious reason for it.

Write down at least five *positive* messages that your subconscious mind has sent you in your life. Think of situations where you did something and then afterward wondered why you did it and couldn't think of a conscious reason for it.

We want to focus on replacing the negative messages with positive messages.

Stop and complete this written exercise before going on!

Be part of the successful 2 percent and complete the exercise now!

I use three methods to communicate with my subconscious. First, I use naps to transfer information into my subconscious. When I was studying to become an accountant, I often got tired and felt that my brain was full and couldn't absorb one more piece of information. So I would put my head down on the desk and take a fifteen-minute nap. When I woke up, it was like I was just waking up first thing in the morning. I felt completely rested, and my conscious mind felt completely empty so I could continue to study and absorb more information.

The second method I use to communicate with my subconscious mind is meditation, a very important part of using our minds to their full potential. Meditation is nothing more than concentrating on a certain subject for an extended period of time. In our country, we tend to think for a very brief period and then move forward. But meditation requires thinking about something for a longer time. Done correctly, it involves both the conscious and subconscious minds working in harmony. The result is usually a far better understanding of the subject on which we are meditating.

The third method I use is to listen to my subconscious mind. I believe strongly that what we put into our mind consciously, especially late at night, is what our subconscious mind works with while we're asleep. Our dreams are nothing but our subconscious mind working out how ideas fit together. Therefore, to use this to our advantage, we can think about a problem that we're trying to solve. Just before going to sleep at night, we can review the problem and all the information related to it and then ask the subconscious mind to work on it. Usually, after doing this for a few days, we will wake up with the answer to the problem. Often we wouldn't have thought of this solution by working it out consciously.

Spirit

We communicate with our Spirit through prayer and meditation. Prayer isn't just something we do at church, and it doesn't have to be long and involved or spoken in Latin or King James English. Prayer is any communication that we have directly with the Spirit that resides inside of each of us. Some common names for it are the Spirit, the Holy Ghost, the Holy Spirit, the Divine Spark, the true self, the inner self, the Source, and the Center. Whatever you call it, recognize that it exists and is important to your success in life. Spirit is where you develop faith and beliefs and values. Spirit is what gives us our sense of what is right and wrong.

How does Spirit affect us in everyday life? Let's say we're studying for the CPA exams. If we believe we can pass, then we can pass. But if we believe we'll fail, then we'll fail. Amazingly, what we believe about ourselves will come true. Even though negative thoughts may have been planted in our subconscious minds by our parents when we were children, we don't have to continue to listen to those thoughts. Our Spirit comes from God, and it tells us the truth if we will take the time to listen to it. When I was preparing for my CPA exams, my subconscious mind as well as my family and friends were telling me that passing was impossible, that I couldn't do it because the CPA exams were very difficult. Based on my track record in academics, I should have listened to them and done something else. But I didn't because my Spirit was telling me that I could do anything I chose to do and that I was worthy of such a success. If my Spirit hadn't told me all these positive messages, my life would be much different today.

Prayer is talking to our Spirit, and meditation is listening to it. When we pray, we talk to our Spirit, tell it what's going on, and ask it questions. When we meditate, or concentrate on something for an extended period, we communicate with our subconscious mind and our Spirit. We listen to what they have to say. I believe that our Spirit is stronger than our subconscious. If the two are at odds with each other, problems will result. For example, my Spirit overrode my subconscious when I was studying for my CPA exams. But long term, this difference couldn't work. I had to work hard to bring the two into alignment.

An excellent example of what this conflict between the subconscious mind and the Spirit can do was illustrated in the movie *Shine* starring Geoffrey Rush. This is the true story of David Holfgott, a world famous classical pianist. The main character, David, was born to a father who had been in a Nazi concentration camps during World War II. In that environment, a person didn't want to get noticed for anything, good or bad, because it could easily lead to his death.

However, the son was gifted to be a great pianist and found his gift early in life. He went against his father's wishes and went off to be a famous pianist in London. However, while his Spirit was leading him to be an inspired pianist, his subconscious mind still held the negative programming that his father had given him. Eventually he was unable to perform on stage. The two were in such strong opposition that he had a mental and emotional breakdown and couldn't play for years.

Inspiration is such an important part of our lives, but we often don't think about where it comes from or how to find it. We won't find it in our bodies or in our minds, but we will find it in our Spirits. If we think about some of the great accomplishments in history, we see that people were inspired to do things that seemed impossible at the time. Michelangelo, who painted the ceiling of the Sistine Chapel in Rome, was a man who was truly inspired. He worked for years under strenuous circumstances, but now people come from all over the world to see his work. Upon seeing the Sistine Chapel it is clear that he was truly inspired. That inspiration came from the Spirit inside of him.

Summary

Communication with the body, the mind, and the Spirit is vital to our success in life. If we use only one or two parts of this triad, we won't reach our full potential. But if we harness all three, we'll reach a level of success that we could not have imagined earlier in our lives.

This chapter talked about the relationship among the three facets of our being. The next three chapters will discuss each facet individually and how each one works in our lives. I feel that this is the foundation of a successful life. *While goals give us the direction in our lives, these three facets of our being are the foundation that we must understand and utilize because they give us the power to achieve our goals.*

A wonderful book on this subject is *Think and Grow Rich* by Napoleon Hill. It's not a book about making lots of money but about how to achieve success. It's an easy book to read and still very powerful after all these years. It is all about communication among the body, mind, and Spirit and how to maximize our potential.

Chapter 4: Body = Health and Energy

Every Journey Begins with the First Step. For Many People, This First Step Is the Hardest to Take

Good Health Is Freedom and Energy

The idea that good health gives us freedom and energy seems like such a simple one. However, many of us in North America don't seem to realize it. Did people who became obese have obesity as their goal in life? How about drug addicts or alcoholics, was acquiring that addiction their goal in life? If we don't define what success is in the area of health, we can easily get into trouble. We live in a country of excesses and are constantly bombarded with messages that tempt us to get involved in unhealthy habits. Just think of these messages that we see every day:

- Beer commercials picture healthy, beautiful young people having lots of fun. They don't show the alcoholic living on the street because he can't hold down a job.
- Commercials and movies depict cigarettes as sexy, but there's nothing sexy about kissing a smoker or dying of lung cancer.

- Food for kids is usually advertised as tasting good and being fun. Food for dogs and cats is usually shown as being healthy and nutritious. As a result, we have a country full of healthy pets with shiny fur and a lot of children with weight and health problems.
- Commercials can persuade people with medical problems that the solution is easy: they can just take a pill.
- Car commercials say that a new car will make you happy and attract friends and maybe a lover. But years of payments on a depreciating vehicle add stress to life and often relationships. Car payments can start a person down the road to personal debt.

Selling unhealthy products can be very profitable, so lots of companies promote these products.

When we're encouraged to purchase a food product, the promoter doesn't always have our best interest at heart. Few advertise eating properly because there's less profit in it. Food companies make more profit if we buy more food. Many foods in America contain sugar or high fructose corn syrup (even worse than sugar), which the majority of Americans are addicted to (yes, addicted!). Diet companies succeed if we fail, are they truly interested in our success? Alcohol and cigarette companies do much better when we do worse.

We don't see many advertisements for eating whole grains, eating healthy, or becoming a vegetarian or vegan. Attitudes in our country are so skewed that people who are overweight are normal and people with healthy habits are considered *health nuts*. If we want to be healthy, we must figure out how to do so for ourselves and avoid societal peer pressure and potential ostracization by many people. When we travel, it can be difficult to find healthy food choices.

But it can be done. Being healthy is certainly possible. It's very easy in this age of information to find out how to live a healthy life by simply adopting a few good habits and sticking to them. This doesn't mean going on a diet and doing without for the rest of our lives. It means eating what we want, but doing so in a way that keeps us healthy and well.

Chapter 4: Body = Health and Energy

Maintaining a healthy weight is simple. Calories in must not exceed calories out. In other words, what we eat each day must only be equivalent to what we use up that day. Unfortunately, while the concept may be simple, putting it into practice may not be easy.

Good health gives us freedom. For example, regular exercise makes it easy to walk, get in and out of cars or planes, play with our children or grandchildren, participate in many hobbies, and many other activities. This is especially true as people age. Also, healthy eating means fewer health problems and less time spent at doctors' offices. It is amazing how eating properly will make us feel better as well as maintain a healthy weight. It is actually easy to maintain good health if we set that as a priority.

Even though many Americans are very concerned about health care, they don't seem to care about their health. *If we spent a little more effort on good health and therefore the prevention of bad health, we would need health care less.*

Personal Growth Exercise:

This exercise helps you become aware of your weaknesses or addictions. Take a few minutes and write down what you might be addicted to. If you say you're not addicted to anything, ask yourself these questions:

Could I go one month without eating sugar?
Could I go one month without drinking alcohol?
Could I go one month without smoking?
Could I go one month without taking non-prescribed drugs?
Could I go one month without watching television?
Could I go one month without (fill in the blank)?

Now describe how much this addiction affects your life.
Does it cause you health issues?
Does it affect your studies or your job?
Does it affect your relationships?
Does it affect your attitude?

Stop and complete this written exercise before going on!

Be part of the successful 2 percent and complete the exercise now!

Many books have been written about health, eating, and exercise. My best advice to you is to keep it simple and always keep having a healthy body as your goal. A healthy body will mean more energy and fewer health problems. People often say they don't have time to exercise and eat right. Well, they seem to find the time for doctor visits when their health fails. For example Brian, a salesman, never took time for good health. But he was constantly sick, missing work and unable to do other things because of bad health. He made many visits to the doctor each year. The lesson here is that by spending a little time now on health, we will enjoy our lives more and save lots of time and cost later on.

What does a healthy life look like? There are two important aspects to maintaining good health: (1) eating and (2) exercising. You can maintain good health by following good eating habits and getting regular exercise.

Eat to Be Healthy

The following list contains good eating behaviors to follow:

- Eat whole grains for breakfast
- Eat mostly vegetables during the day, preferably raw or steamed
- Eat fruit for snacks
- Eat four to six small meals or snacks daily
- Drink lots of water

- Finish eating and drinking liquids before seven o'clock in the evening (three to four hours before bedtime)
- Avoid fad diets
- Change your attitude toward food. Seek good nutrition instead of pleasure
- Don't punish yourself for overeating or eating the wrong things; just try to do better tomorrow
- Read books about health and nutrition
- Consider the benefits of fasting with the help of a medical professional
- Use the 80/20 rule (explained in the following paragraph)

Let's begin with the Pareto Principle or the 80/20 rule, which applies to many situations in business. The rule states that 80 percent of a business's profits come from 20 percent of its activity. In addition, 80 percent of its problems come from 20 percent of its customers. If we think about our own lives, there are many areas where this might apply. For example, I spent 80 percent of my time as a professor with 20 percent of my students, who were having problems.

How can we apply this rule to eating and exercising to be healthy? One of the reasons that people fail or don't even try to be healthier is that they feel that they must be perfect 100 percent of the time. Not true! We need to do the things that will make us healthy most of the time (80 percent), but we have the leeway to not follow these habits part of the time (20 percent). If we do the right thing 80 percent of the time (five or six days a week) and fall off for 20 percent of the time (one or two days a week), we will end up healthier. What we will discover is that after awhile, healthy eating will become a habit that we enjoy, so we'll be less likely to want to stray from the path.

When I started to become more concerned about my health, I talked to my daughter, who is my health guru, and she told me about whole grains. I had always enjoyed vegetables and fruits; they were the mainstay of my eating. However, in the morning, I always ate boxed cereals. It was scary to read the labels because they indicated that the cereals had many bad things in them, especially sugar in its various forms. Once I switched to preparing whole grains for breakfast, my weight dropped. I felt much better because I had stopped taking all those bad chemicals and sugar into my body and instead was eating very healthy food with lots of nutrients and fiber. Whole grains are inexpensive, easy to prepare and can be purchased at many health food stores. I now have the philosophy that I don't want to eat anything that is already prepared and comes in a box or a can. I prefer not to eat processed foods.

When I was in my twenties I would eat a breakfast that contained sugar. Eating cereal with sugar or toast with jam or jelly for breakfast would cause an energy surge called a *sugar high*. However, later in the day, when the sugar high was gone, I would crave more sugar to replace it. This created an energy roller coaster of sugar highs followed by crashes and strong cravings.

Many people in our country seem obsessed with dieting and losing weight. Diets, temporary changes in eating habits, are often an unbalanced, unnatural way of eating and don't work in the long term. So, never diet!

Personal Growth Exercise:

Before you go on, take a few minutes to write responses to these prompts about eating habits.

1) Describe how you feel about your current weight. Men tend to be optimistic and women tend to be pessimistic when it comes to their weight.
2) List five things that you can start doing today to improve your eating habits so you'll be healthier. Don't list "go on a diet" which is a drastic change. Instead, list ways to amend eating habits a little bit at a time. Review this list often.
3) Check your Body Mass Index (BMI). This can be found on the internet. What does your BMI indicate?
4) If you're having a problem with your eating habits, try the exercise at the end of chapter 2 to make a change in the next thirty days.

Stop and complete this written exercise before going on!

Be part of the successful 2 percent and complete the exercise now!

Exercise to be Healthy

The following list contains good exercise behaviors to follow:

- Exercise to maintain flexibility, muscle tone, and a strong heart
- Perform basic exercises for fifteen to thirty minutes, three to five times a week
- Perform aerobic exercises for at least thirty minutes, three to five times a week
- Don't try to lose weight through exercise alone. Weight loss is best accomplished by exercise combined with a change in eating habits
- Learn how to breathe properly using your diaphragm
- Read books on physical fitness
- Walk for at least one hour a day

I could spend a thousand pages talking about exercise, but I just want to describe a simple plan that we can follow at home with a small outlay of cash. We don't need gym memberships and fancy workout clothes to be healthy. All we need is to make exercise a priority in our lives. However, if a health club makes that easier for you, then by all means go for it.

Personally, I've never liked structured exercise programs. I have kept in shape all my life simply by being physically active. I hike, ride my bike, and walk every chance I get. This always seemed to be enough. All my life I tried to eat healthy foods but was loose about following a particular plan. This worked for me most of my life, but I noticed that as I age, two things are happening. First, I am gaining a little weight and second, I am getting less flexible and my muscles less toned.

Concerning the issue of flexibility and muscle tone, I thought of my former boss in California. I went to visit him when he was in his seventies, and he told me that he went to the gym to work out daily. I was surprised because I wondered why a man in his seventies would want to have really big muscles. He said that he wasn't trying to build muscle; he was just trying to keep what he already had. Flexibility is also a real issue as we age, so there is a real advantage to exercising.

I like to spend time exercising because I find the rhythm of repetitions is very peaceful and relaxing. In addition afterward I feel extremely energized. I decided to design a simple exercise plan that I could do at home. Home is more comfortable than a gym, and exercising at home saves lots of time.

You should keep exercise simple. In his book, *Body for Life*, Bill Phillips gives examples of exercise programs. Bill Phillips is a bodybuilder but I don't go for the bodybuilding part of his book. However, the advice is very good for improving fitness. I do some of the exercises he recommends three to five days a week. It has done wonders for my flexibility and muscle tone.

Each day I vary which exercises I do and how many I do. The total cost of my exercise program was less than a hundred dollars, which included the book and a simple set of free weights. Remember to start off slowly and build up gradually. Unless we're planning to enter a bodybuilding contest, we have no reason to get buff. All we want is to get toned as part of being healthy.

Want to know something amazing? All my life I hated running, but a few years ago I had an uncontrollable urge to run. Now I love running. I run three times a week for between fifteen and twenty miles each week. I have run a half marathon, and eventually I want to run a full marathon. My running is truly unbelievable to me. I never thought that I could run these distances and really enjoy them.

Personal Growth Exercise:

Before you go on, take a few minutes to review your exercise activity.

1) Describe how you feel about your flexibility, muscle tone, and heart health.
2) How often do you exercise?
3) List five things you can do starting today to exercise better.
4) If you're having a problem getting started with an exercise program, try the exercise at the end of chapter 2 to make a change in the next thirty days.

Warning: exercise can cause weight gain. Here is a trap that people like me sometimes fall into after exercising: we feel that we just had a great workout and burned off a lot of calories, so we believe that we can now go to the coffee shop and have a latte and a sweet. The bad news is that the snack we consume contains more calories than what we just burned off. I gained weight when I started running, and it definitely was not all muscle. As you lose fat and gain muscle, weight lose may seem slow – but muscle mass is desirable weight.

Stop and complete this written exercise before going on!

Be part of the successful 2 percent and complete the exercise now!

Summary

Sensible eating and exercise work hand in hand to keep us healthy. If we eat more vegetables and fruits and fewer processed foods, we can maintain the right weight and be healthier. Regular exercise has lots of health benefits also. The greatest benefit of exercise may not be physical but the wonderful change in attitude.

Chapter 5: Mind = Knowledge, Discipline, and Wisdom

You Are Unique, Just Like Everyone Else

When we refer to our mind, we are considering our brain, the thinking process, our will, and our emotions. We will look at them as one since they operate together.

Knowledge

I believe that our minds are our greatest underutilized assets. We could do so much more if we could only reach a greater usage of our brains' potential. I believe that a lot of the great people in history did amazing things because they found a way to use a larger percentage of their brains' power.

There's an old saying that an idle mind is the devil's playground. This relates to the unused portion of the brain. Since we are not using our minds to their capacity, there's a lot of extra activity going on that doesn't necessarily work for our benefit. It has always amazed me that we humans seem designed with evil as our default setting. If we leave kids alone for a while, what happens? They often get into trouble. If we leave teenagers alone without anything to do, what happens? They often get into trouble. This even applies to adults. If we don't have enough to do, we often end up getting into trouble. It seems to me that we have to work at being good and leading a good life.

On the other hand, if we use our minds more fully, it is amazing what we can accomplish. I know I've done things that have amazed me. In high school I felt that I couldn't accomplish much or learn hard subjects like calculus and physics. To my surprise, I ended up becoming an accountant in Canada and later in California. I took the exams in both countries and passed them the first time. I earned a bachelor's degree and a master's degree and went on to be a professor for twenty-five years. I feel that I figured out how to use more of my mind's potential. *I believe that anyone can do amazing things if they want and are willing to apply themselves.*

I truly believe that we can do almost anything we put our minds to. When I started in junior high school, I had a terrible attitude problem. In high school I had an even worse attitude problem. I just was not a happy camper and I did not want to be there. This was all related to my childhood home being a place that would make a person crazy. My attitude didn't improve when I got to university, but I still managed to pass all of my courses, even if just barely. After I graduated from university, I felt lost and didn't know what I wanted to do. I was bored and wanted some direction in life, so I took some night classes at a local university.

When I took accounting, I felt like I had just hit a home run: I found what I was destined to do. I had always enjoyed math and was good at it, so accounting was a great fit. But even more than that was how accounting was set up. In grade eight I had a business mowing lawns. I established a set of books to keep track of my income and expenses. I put the expenses on the left and the income on the right. The difference between the two columns was my profit. I had designed this as a teenager all by myself. I was amazed to learn that that's exactly how accounting systems are set up in business. I felt completely at home with this subject.

In my twenties, I quit my job as an officer in the Canadian Navy and took a position as an accountant in training with a fifty percent pay cut. This was a job that I really loved. Since I never thought that I was smart, I worked hard. I realized that I didn't

Chapter 5: Mind = Knowledge, Discipline, and Wisdom

really know how to study, so I approached some really good students and asked them how they studied. They told me their techniques, and I used them. In accountancy classes, I was usually in the top five on exams, and I was one of the top students overall in our finals. I averaged 90 percent on my CPA exams, which the majority of students don't even pass.

I had the ability, talent, skill, aptitude, whatever you want to call it inside me all along. It was only when I started studying accounting that I tapped into it. What if I had never taken that night class and discovered my desire to do accounting? It is important to know that we already have everything inside us that we need to live fulfilling lives. We just have to *discover* it and then *develop* it.

Now, you may be saying that I was lucky to find my talent. You're right that I was lucky because it has made all the difference in my life. But I didn't just stumble upon it one day while I was walking aimlessly through life. I was in a job that I really disliked and wanted to leave, so I had to ask, for what other job? I took classes at university for a few years without success until I found the accounting class.

Later I had the knowledge and the desire to teach, but I was completely incapable of talking in front of a group of people. You may feel uncomfortable with public speaking, but I was absolutely terrified. An opportunity came up with a group called Toastmasters who teach people how to speak in public. Within eight weeks I was leading the meeting and enjoying every minute of it. Once again, this wasn't some great feat that I accomplished. It was something inside of me that I *discovered* and *developed*. This led me to be what God had designed me to be, a teacher.

Mental Food and Exercise

Just like our bodies need to be fed and exercised, our minds need to be fed and exercised also. Many people do this only when forced to. Often people stop learning after they leave school. If we do that, we will severely limit our lives. Instead, we should learn new things all the time about work, personal growth, hobbies, relationships, and anything else. We have to guard against being passive and watching too much television. When we do watch television, we see someone else live life while we're not living ours. I understand that we might like something on television, but it just doesn't make sense to spend so much time watching others. I get a kick out of the reality shows. Some people go on an adventure, and we get to watch. *It would be better if we got up and went out on our own adventure!*

What do our minds like to eat? Lots! Our minds are hungry and want to be fed. If we don't feed them good stuff, they'll be eating junk food. We could listen to a motivational speaker or read books that will teach us new things. If we aren't doing something constructive instead of watching television, our minds are digesting commercials and the lessons in the television shows. We will not lead happy, successful lives if we fill our minds with these ideas. Remember *garbage in, garbage out.*

People always argue that there are some good shows on television. I could argue that there is some good stuff in the garbage truck also. I don't want it dumped in my yard so I can pick out the good stuff because I'll also be stuck with all the bad stuff. Do you feel that the time you spend watching television is spent wisely? We need to consider how our lives could be changed if we reduced the time we spend watching television.

I have heard people say that they watch four to six hours of television a day. That is one-third of the time that we're awake each day. What do we gain from this huge time investment? Are our lives any richer? What else could we be doing with that time? We could earn a university degree. We could be involved in our favorite hobbies. We could volunteer at our church or in a community activity. Just think that if we reduced our television viewing by half, we could use that time to do something that would enrich our lives.

The garbage in, garbage out idea also applies to reading. There are a lot of good books from which we can learn something and that will inspire us in some way. Choose books that will motivate you.

Chapter 5: Mind = Knowledge, Discipline, and Wisdom

I recommend that we decide to learn something new and then make it a goal and focus on achieving that goal. One time in my life when I felt particularly lost, I set the goal of getting my MBA. That goal spurred my mind, and not only did I get an MBA, but I also got a CPA license and a new life in California. For years I've read self-help books, listened to motivational speakers, and read my Bible regularly. I have also avoided watching television most of my life. All of this feeding of my mind has been wonderful—it's made my life much richer.

Next let's look at exercising our minds. *Like our bodies, our minds need to be fed and exercised.* How do we exercise our minds? Use them! How we do that depends on our stage of life and what else is going on in our lives. We can take a degree or just take a course that interests us. We can find a hobby we're interested in. We can learn just for fun. Speaking another language is a valuable skill to learn. Most people in the world speak more than one language. What about playing a musical instrument? The opportunities are endless.

We can join a book club or Bible study that requires us to read, think, and then talk about what we read. Reading in this way is more challenging than just reading a novel. Some people do crossword puzzles or Sudoku to keep their minds sharp.

Many people lack the self-discipline to set up a program of study and then follow it, but there are many preset programs they can take advantage of. We could check out a community college, community center, recreation department, or the Internet. If we commit ourselves to learning and doing our absolute best, we may change our lives in ways we never dreamed we would.

Remember the theory of Earl Nightingale that if you do something for one hour a day, in three years you will be an expert at it. Just think what would happen if you gave up one hour of television a day and devoted that hour to something you wanted to accomplish. You could learn how to play a musical instrument, speak a new language, or do anything you desire.

You might think this doesn't sound like a great deal of fun. We can still do the things that we like; all I'm suggesting is that we spend some time on improving our health and our minds.

The rewards will far outweigh the costs in the long run. Besides, learning something that you want to learn is fun!

Discipline

Our brains have awesome potential. When we get to later chapters, we'll see that a great deal of our potential is centered in our minds. One of the greatest ways our minds can unleash our potential is to provide discipline. *Self-discipline is simply doing what we should do even when it's not what we want to do.* I know that many people in our society don't like external discipline. Internal discipline, or self-discipline, is even more difficult. To discipline ourselves is hard because we typically rebel against external discipline, so when we attempt self-discipline, we rebel against ourselves. That is why many people fall down when it comes to self-discipline.

Have you heard of the "Law of Liberty"? I know that sounds like a paradox because the word *law* usually means a restriction of freedom. *The Law of Liberty refers to self-discipline, or restricting what we do in one part of life so that we have more freedom in another part.*

For example, if we don't do drugs, we give up that freedom because we want to be free from the consequences of drug use, including the complete loss of freedom. Do you know anyone who has used drugs for a long time and who has freedom in his or her life? The same is true with food, alcohol, sex, pornography, television, the Internet, and anything else when used to excess. If we don't exercise self-discipline, these habits can take over our lives. There's often a fine line between enjoying something and being addicted to it.

Another important area of our lives is financial freedom. We have the freedom to borrow and buy far more than is reasonable for us. If we exercise self-discipline in financial matters, we will be free to do what we can afford. If we don't exercise self-discipline in this area, we end up with excessive debt and the inability to repay it. That is a real loss of freedom.

How do we develop self-discipline? I believe that it comes from a strong desire to accomplish something. If we set a goal, either formally or informally, and we have a strong desire to achieve that goal, we will have self-discipline. Look at professional athletes: many of them exhibit poor self-discipline off the field, getting into all kinds of trouble. But on the field, they exhibit good self-discipline because they really want to be successful at their sport. It really stands out if an athlete shows poor self-discipline on the playing field.

I believe that we can develop self-discipline just like any other habit. To improve my self-discipline, I read a lot of motivational books. They talk about how to use your mind to improve your life. They help me know how to think, how to set goals, how to motivate myself, how to follow a plan, and how to modify the plan or a behavior if it needs to change.

The mind is much more powerful than most people realize. *What you believe has great power.* For example, I have always believed that I won't get sick. By sick I mean colds, flu and seasonal illnesses. I have this as a firm belief, and it has held true for my whole life. In the past thirty years, I have not missed a single day of work or play due to illness. When I was teaching, I typically had about 150 students in my classes from all over the world who were often sick with colds, the flu, and heaven only knows what else. Yet in twenty-five years of teaching, I never missed a day due to illness. Why? I simply don't believe in it.

I have a friend who believes that she will get a cold each winter. She further believes that the cold will take ten days to come on, be around for ten days, and take ten days to leave, for a total of thirty days with the cold. When she first feels sick, she has it in her mind that the cold is going to last thirty days. Guess what—it lasts thirty days. What you put into your mind and what you believe will be what you experience in life.

I recently read a book called *The Biology of Belief* by Bruce H. Lipton that validates this belief. People have often scoffed at me when I tell them I don't believe in getting sick. But this book states that the medical community is coming to realize that the very cells in our body will respond to what we believe and change and make it come true. Because I believed I wouldn't get sick, my body responded in such a way as to prevent me from getting sick. Conversely, my friend's body responded by letting her get sick for thirty days each winter.

I believe that when a medicine works, its effects are partly due to our minds and partly due to the chemicals themselves. We've all heard stories about studies in which patients were given a placebo and did every bit as well as people who took medicines. Why do flu shots work? I think that often they work because people who get them *believe* that they're protected. Why don't some flu shots work? I think some people still get the flu even after the flu shot because their belief that they'll get the flu is stronger than their belief that the flu shot will work.

We can program our minds that we can do whatever we want to do. Can we be healthy? Yes. Can we give up a bad habit? Yes. Can we have the career of our dreams? Yes. Can we find the soul mate that we have always longed for? Yes. I firmly believe that we can do almost anything we want with our minds.

Personal Growth Exercise:

Describe how you feed your mind:
Do you read books that help you learn more about your career or hobbies?
Do you attend seminars where you learn a new skill?
Do you pollute your mind with gossip (e.g., from tabloids)?
Do you pollute your mind with television?
Do you pollute your mind with bad news?

Stop and complete this written exercise before going on!

Be part of the successful 2 percent and complete the exercise now!

Chapter 5: Mind = Knowledge, Discipline, and Wisdom

We Become What We Think

One of the great beliefs of scholars, philosophers, and prophets throughout history has been that *we become what we think about.* This is both powerful and scary. It states that we have control over our lives. Each of us is the only one who controls our thoughts (unless we give that power away to someone else), and our thoughts are what we become.

The mind is to the body as a pilot is to a plane. The pilot is the brain that controls and directs the plane. He can make it go up or down, east or west, and take off and land safely. Plane crashes often happen because the pilot wasn't doing what he was supposed to be doing.

Our minds work the same way in our lives. If we fill our minds with good material, then they have good thoughts and attitudes, and we experience good outcomes in our lives. However, if we fill our minds with bad material, then we have bad thoughts and attitudes, and we experience bad outcomes in life. It is not what happens to us in life but how we perceive and respond to what happens to us that will determine how happy we are.

Our minds are powerful tools. Most of us use a small fraction of their capacity. The mind is a tool that we can use to change our lives. Let's do it!

Just think about it: we have the power to determine our level of happiness. That is an awesome power and a huge responsibility. It doesn't come naturally. We must learn how to do it properly.

We enter the world as babies screaming and demanding what we want when we want it. We reach maturity when we learn to balance our lives and as adults we are not still screaming and demanding what we want.

Wisdom

Usually we think that wisdom comes with age because we must first gather information and organize it into knowledge. Then, we must have life experiences, both positive and negative, to help us learn how to use the knowledge we possess. My definition of *wisdom is the application of knowledge to a given situation.* I think that's accurate. I also believe that the ability to apply knowledge comes from our life experiences. Wisdom seems to come with age simply because we gain more knowledge and experience the older we get. However, some younger individuals are wise while some older individuals are not. Wisdom doesn't come automatically as we age.

I believe that gaining wisdom is an admirable goal. Getting an education and gaining knowledge are great, but if we can't apply what we learn to our lives, what's the purpose? Some entrepreneurs don't have a great education, but they're successful because they learned what they needed to know and were very good at applying it to their lives. For example, I studied what made some businesspeople successful. One of the most important determining factors was their ability to pick the right people for the job. This ability comes from wisdom.

We all have wisdom to some degree. We can break wisdom down into many categories, two of which are worldly wisdom and Godly wisdom. The more worldly wisdom we have, the more financially successful we will be. However, the more Godly wisdom we possess, the more peace, joy, and contentment we will experience. A balance between the two is best.

Summary

Why don't we use more of our mind's capacity? It is baffling to me why people don't seem to want to use more of their brain capacity. It is free, has unlimited potential, and can make unbelievable changes in our lives.

Everyone can use more of their mind. I really encourage you to look into what you would like to do with your mind. I'm sure the rewards will surprise you.

Just like our physical bodies our minds need to be fed and exercised or they will atrophy. If we make a conscious effort to feed our minds good material daily, it will improve our attitude immensely. If we exercise our minds not only will they be stronger but our lives will expand with the new things undertaken.

Discipline sounds like a bad word to many people, but a little self-discipline will change our lives dramatically and give us more freedom. The more you use self-discipline and see the benefits, the easier it'll be to use it in other situations as well.

Chapter 6: Spirit = Belief, Faith, Confidence, and Inspiration

Obedience to God is the Key to a Life of Blessing

Belief

Believing something and working toward it will make it come to be. I remember trying out for the football team in high school. I was asked to try out because of my size. However, I believed that I wouldn't make it because I wasn't competitive and didn't like football all that much. I probably didn't put my heart into the try out. At that time, I also had a job that I felt was important. I feel my desire to keep my job may have been stronger than my desire to play football. I remember talking one day with a friend who was also trying out. We weren't doing all that well. He was so gung-ho and fired up I couldn't believe it. I asked him how long he planned to stick around. I told him that if I made the team, I was going to stay until the first game. If I didn't get picked to play, then I planned to quit. He said that he wasn't ever going to quit, that he was going to keep trying out until he made the team. Well, it's probably no surprise that I quit and went to work and that he stayed and eventually ended up playing.

The different parts of Spirit listed in the chapter title are overlapping. However, I feel that they each deserve a separate discussion. Belief is a powerful part of our success, and when we get to the *Rocks to Diamonds* part of the book, we'll see how important a part it is. *Belief underlies self-confidence and inspiration; it's a very important element for our success.*

Let's look at how belief is a key element when we're learning a new skill like driving a car. When we learned to drive, the first time out, we were probably nervous and afraid to make a mistake. But after that first time out, when we had success and didn't hit anything, our belief in our ability to drive rose and so did our self-confidence. Each time we went out driving, our belief that we could do this rose and our self-confidence rose with it. Eventually we got to the point where our belief in our ability to drive switched to a *certainty*, and then we drove without really having to think about what we were doing.

What if we could raise our level of belief to certainty without repeated small successes to increase our self-confidence? This would be a major leap forward. Well, that's what we will discuss in chapter 11. The better we can accomplish this, the faster we'll grow in whatever it is we're doing. Raising our belief to certainty is a key part of the *Rocks to Diamonds* program.

When I first started playing golf, I read an article about Jack Nicklaus, one of the greatest golfers of all time. People always wanted to know the secret to his great success. One of his secrets was that he would play the entire course in his mind until he developed the certainty that he knew how to play it best. He would picture every shot in detail and see himself making the shot. Then he would picture the ball landing where he wanted it to. Before he even stepped onto the golf course for the first time, he was certain that he could play it well, and he usually did just that.

We can do that with almost anything. If we're starting to teach, we can picture ourselves giving a lecture with confidence and answering all our students' questions. When we enter the classroom, we'll be certain of success. When I'm going to perform in a play, I spend part of my rehearsal time picturing myself delivering my lines with ease and the audience's reaction. If I am going to give a speech, I picture past successes and then see myself giving my next speech successfully.

Chapter 6: Spirit = Belief, Faith, Confidence, and Inspiration

Do you believe visualization works? Often we use this technique backward, and unfortunately, it works both ways. Let's say that we have to give a speech in front of a lot of people. (Public speaking is one of the most feared things that someone has to do in life. Public speaking often ranks above death when peoples' fears are studied.) What do most people do? They picture in their mind the speech that they're to give. But instead of picturing success, they picture failure. They see themselves forgetting everything that they wanted to say and standing there lost and tongue tied. What happens? They do exactly what they pictured, and then they have a new belief that they can't speak in public, and their self-confidence decreases as a result. Their poor result reinforces the negative belief, so their performance gets worse as time goes on.

Visualization is a powerful tool that we can use for or against ourselves. Why not use it to our advantage?

One belief that I assume you hold is a belief in God. If you don't believe in God, please keep an open mind and consider what I'm saying. Many successful people believe in God and base their lives upon that belief. I was very anti-church, but I've always believed in God. At age thirty-five, I went back to church and started to learn more about God, and it made a huge difference in my life. If you don't believe in God, I believe you're missing the most important part of life.

When I was thirty-five, I hadn't been to church in over twenty years. When I started going again, I participated in a Bible study and met a man who explained it like this: if you believe in God and there is no God, you will have a better life here on earth and nothing will happen when you die. But if you don't believe in God and there is a God, then you'll have a worse life here on earth, and when you die, you'll live forever in hell. I'm not trying to threaten but just to point out that belief in God and following God's teachings will make our lives here on earth a whole lot better. The teachings in the Bible show us how to live successful lives and how to be happy.

Think of God as the perfect parent who only wants us to be happy and successful. To that end, God instructs us what we should do to have a better life in the Bible, His instruction book for life. The closer we follow its rules, the better our lives will be. Just think if the only laws in the country were the Ten Commandments (see Appendix B) and if everyone followed them. There would be no crime or conflict. People would get along well, and everyone would be happy. When we watch or read the news and see wars and criminal activity, most of the actions we see are violations of the Ten Commandments. Jesus said, "*Love others as you love yourself.*" If everyone followed this, it would immediately eliminate the need for the justice system.

God is like electricity. God is the energy in our lives. Most people don't understand electricity even though they use it every day, all day. Even though they don't understand it and can't see it, they still believe in it and use it because it allows them to do what they want and have successful lives. If we were not plugged into electricity, we would have no power. But when we are plugged in, we have the power to do whatever we want.

To take advantage of electricity, we must take action to get ourselves connected. God powers our lives through the Spirit inside us, like the wires in our houses. *If we get connected to the Spirit within us, we will have unlimited power in our lives.*

To connect an appliance to electricity, we use an electrical plug with three prongs. God also has three prongs, or parts: Father, Son, and Holy Spirit, each one distinct yet all part of one. The Spirit, which resides inside of us, is by far the most powerful of the three elements of our being: mind, body, and Spirit. As I discussed in chapter 3, combining the three elements yields the greatest power. Remember we said that we could assign weights to the three elements. If we give the body a weight of 10, then the mind would have a weight of 100, and the Spirit, being the most powerful, would have a weight of 1,000. When we combine all three, we get:

Body x Mind x Spirit = Power
10 x 100 x 1,000 = 1,000,000

A person who uses all three parts in this way is really alive and strongly inspired. Think of a very high achiever's performance compared to an average person's; the difference is enormous. My point is not to argue for a specific value for each element but to illustrate that the mind is so much more powerful than the body and that the Spirit is so much more powerful than the mind. If we want to achieve something great in life, we must combine all three.

For example, let's look at an athlete. An athlete who uses only her body could score goals in the weekend pick-up game. However, a lot of athletes have strong physical skills, so an athlete using only her body would not stand out in a crowd. But if the athlete uses her mind as well as her body, then she will be a much better player and maybe go on to lead her team to the state championship in high school. But to be a top performer, the athlete must also engage her Spirit to also have the inspiration to perform so highly. This might lead to an Olympic gold medal.

Let's examine this amazing gift of the Holy Spirit more closely. The Spirit is inside every one of us, and we can communicate with it through prayer. When we do, we receive:

- Faith that we're doing what God designed us to do
- Confidence in ourselves and our abilities
- The belief that we can achieve what we set out to do
- Inspiration that gives us the unfathomable energy and burning desire to succeed
- Strength to develop and exercise self-discipline

Faith

One of the greatest motivators in my life has been faith that what I'm doing is God's will for me. This may sound strange to you, but when I was a child of about five, God spoke to me and told me that I was to be a teacher. As an adult, when I was a professor, every day that I went into class, I remembered that this was what God wanted me to do. Every day before class, I prayed that God would guide me to do His will and not let my ego get in the way. As a result, the classes that I taught were just amazing to me. My evaluations from students indicated they felt the same way. That was one place in life where I felt I was in the zone, like I was suspended from myself and was gliding along on God's power.

When students asked me questions, I would answer with an example that I had never thought of before and sometimes didn't know that I knew. But it would be the perfect example for the situation. I've not been blessed with a lot of patience, but in the classroom, I exhibited patience that astounded me.

Do you know what it is like to be operating in your purpose? An excellent example is seen in the movie *Billy Elliot* about a boy who wanted to be a ballet dancer but grew up in a coal mining town. At one point, Billy is asked what it's like when he dances. He responds that it's like he is somewhere else, like electricity is running through his body. When he dances, he's doing exactly what he was designed to do. He had to fight his family and neighborhood to do it, but he did it successfully. He also changed the people around him by showing them his faith in what he was doing. He showed others in his community with less belief in themselves what life could offer them.

Faith is belief in the unseen. Faith isn't just about God but about anything in our lives that we can't see. The biggest unseen part of our lives is our future. We can exercise our faith that we'll have the future we want and change the direction of our lives to be much more fulfilling as we aim for that future.

If we have faith that we'll be a successful athlete, teacher, parent, truck driver, or anything else, then we multiply our chances of success. If we have faith that we'll be a failure, an addict, a prisoner, or homeless, then we'll achieve that instead. Why not pick something wonderful to do with our lives and then live by faith that we'll be successful at it?

Sometimes people are afraid to have faith in themselves or their future. They feel that they don't deserve success or that it will be impossible. Each of us is a child of God, who loves us and wants us to be happy, so we definitely deserve to have a successful future.

Confidence

Confidence comes from knowing that God made us and is with us in all that we do. Spirit gives us self-confidence.

Suppose that we believe God made us perfect human beings and that God loves us and wants us to be happy more than anything else in the whole universe. Think of the self-image and self-confidence we would possess knowing that God made us and loves us no matter what we've ever done in our lives. To me, the greatest message of the Christian church is that God loves us eternally, and God forgives us. Now that is a powerful message.

When I was struggling with my self-image, my therapist told me to write down positive affirmations and to repeat them daily to reprogram my mind. I did this, and it worked—my mind sent me positive messages instead of negative messages. But the mind is like a computer and simply does what it's told without emotion. Reprogramming my mind helped, but it was only part of the change that I needed.

Later, my therapist told me to imagine that God made me and that he wants me to be happy. He said to picture that when I was born, I was a perfect image of God. However, my parents (who were not perfect) raised me, and they unintentionally taught me that I was unworthy and unlovable. I had a choice: I could hold on to the beliefs that my parents taught me, or I could replace them with new beliefs. How wonderful it is to believe that I was created by God in his own image and that he wants me to be all that I can be. Let me tell you that once I changed my beliefs, my self-image changed radically, and my self-confidence went through the roof. If God loves me, then what does it matter what any person thinks about me?

This is an example of how my subconscious mind was in conflict with my Spirit. The conflict lasted for many years in which I struggled to find peace. I knew that I had some kind of disturbance inside, but I didn't know what it was until my therapist helped me. Once I aligned my subconscious mind and my Spirit, my world changed dramatically.

Inspiration

Inspiration comes from our Spirit and gives us the confidence to act on our beliefs. Insecurity is the opposite of inspiration and certainly doesn't lead to much self-confidence. If we are insecure, we doubt our self-worth or our abilities, and we will lack confidence to act on what's inside us. Insecurity causes people to look to things outside themselves to give their lives meaning and purpose. Unfortunately, because many parents don't know how to be good parents, they cause their children to be insecure and to lack the self-confidence to go out into the world on their own.

The most powerful aspect of all that the Spirit gives us is inspiration. A person who is inspired has tons of energy and drive. They have self-confidence, they believe that they're doing what they were designed to do, and they're practically guaranteed to be successful. Don't get in the way of an inspired person because there is no stopping him. Right or wrong, that person will succeed because he's certain that what he's doing is what he was meant to do.

Inspiration plays a big part in finding our purpose in life. If we want to have a significant life, we can do all the research and soul searching in the world, but until we get truly inspired, we won't find our true purpose. Just think of the last time we did something that we were truly inspired to do. We forgot to eat. We forgot the time. We forgot other duties that we were supposed to do because we were just so lost in that activity that the rest of the world ceased to exist to us. When I go to the theater and paint sets, this happens to me. One day I had to paint a scene of a street in London. For about four hours, I was completely lost in the task, and absolutely nothing existed to me except what I was doing. Before I knew it, it was getting late, way past quitting time, and I hadn't eaten or even thought of eating during that time.

Those are the experiences of life that we never forget because we would like to get them back or to duplicate them in some way. I can remember some of those moments from my life. I hope you've had a lot of those moments in your life. We can tap into the power of inspiration and make it happen more often if we want. We just need to get in touch with our Spirit and communicate our desires to find what we were designed to do. Then we listen for the response.

It is important to listen to our Spirit because it will tell us what we need to do rather than what we want to do. We may want to have a great day kayaking tomorrow, but we may not get to do that because the Spirit tells us that we need to spend time with our sick child. If we ignore the Spirit and go kayaking, we may have a terrible time because we're not inspired. On the other hand, if we spend the time with our sick child, we may experience one of the greatest moments in our relationship. We never know when these special moments will come up.

Personal Growth Exercise:

Describe how your Spirit works for you.
Does it give you hope?
Does it give you a sense of self-worth?
Does it give you self-confidence?
Does it inspire you?

Stop and complete this written exercise before going on!

Be part of the successful 2 percent and complete the exercise now!

Summary

Our Spirit is a part of God living inside us. That means that we can directly communicate with God anytime we want to exercise that connection. If God is for us, who can be against us? Just think of that! If part of God lives inside of each of us, and God wants us to be successful in life, all we have to do is learn to be in tune with God to have a wonderful life.

Belief in self is critical to achieving anything in life. This self-confidence will allow us to try new things and grow. Visualization is a wonderful tool for seeing what we want to become.

Our Spirit is also the source of our motivation and inspiration so it is important to be in touch with what is happening in our Spirit.

Chapter 7: Rocks to Diamonds Cycle

*We Should Always Pursue Perfection,
We Just Might Reach Excellence*
Vince Lombardi

This section talks about a simple process that we can use to make changes in our lives. This process works in any part of life where repetition leads to success, such as learning to play the piano or learning to speak Spanish. Anyone familiar with feedback loops will recognize those as the foundation of the *Rocks to Diamonds* Cycle. Rocks represent people when in their raw state, before they've discovered and developed their gifts. Diamonds represent people after they've discovered and developed these gifts. Here are the four steps in the *Rocks to Diamonds* Cycle:

Step 1:

Rocks represent our potential in life. Every single one of us has lots of potential that we don't use. Our bodies could perform at a much higher level than they do now. As we discussed earlier, most of us are not using the full potential of our brain capacity, and we are not engaging our Spirit nearly as much as we could.

Step 2:

Effort is the action we take to use our potential to accomplish the task at hand. We apply our *body, mind,* and *Spirit* as well as we can at that point in our lives. We choose how much effort we exert each day. Since it is our choice, why not choose to give it our all?

Step 3:

Result is the outcome of the effort we applied to our potential. We might think that the more effort we apply, the better the result we would obtain. However, both the quantity and the quality of the effort determine the outcome.

Step 4:

Belief refers to what we believe about ourselves and about our abilities. At step 2, we begin to believe in the result we'll get from step 3. After step 3 is complete, one of three things will happen: our belief in our ability to obtain the desired outcome will increase, decrease, or stay the same.

Repeat Step 1:

We go back to *Rocks*, our potential. Now that we've had experience from going through the previous loop, we can change our performance. If our first run through the loop was successful, our belief in our ability to obtain the desired outcome is now greater, and we will apply that new belief to our potential. Our potential hasn't changed but we now *believe* that we have more potential than before. When we complete another loop, we should see greater results than the previous time.

Repeat Step 2:

We will put forth better *effort* this time because now we are more confident that we will have success in our endeavors. Remember, since success breeds success, we need to challenge ourselves. However, failure breeds failure, so if we had a bad result the first time, we will have to put forth more and better effort this time.

Repeat Step 3:

The *result* will probably be better than before: we're improving. This improvement may be only incremental, but as we complete the cycle more times, the increments add up to a significant improvement. *Never give up!*

Repeat Step 4:

Our *belief* in ourselves will increase further as we see improvement. The ideal outcome is that our belief turns into certainty. Then we will be performing at the highest level and we will truly be "diamonds".

We can continue through the loop as many times as we want or need to. Hopefully, we get better every time we cycle through. There truly is no limit to our success. We might feel that we will reach a limit or know everything that there is to know, but that is simply not true. There is always something new to learn or a different way to do what we are doing. It seemed that I learned something new every day when I was teaching. Most of what I learned was from my students.

The *Rocks to Diamonds Cycle* applies to any situation where we learn through repetition. For example, if we're learning to play a musical instrument, we go through a cycle each time we practice or play. We need to monitor how much effort we're giving and how good that effort is, how the result changed, and how our belief in our ability improves with practice. The old saying "practice makes perfect" is wrong. The correct saying is, "perfect practice makes perfect." If we practice poorly, then we'll learn to play poorly. So each time we practice, we should give a great performance and always put forth our best effort.

We need to ensure that we do not become discouraged by setbacks. We must make sure that a bad day doesn't get us off track. A bad cycle doesn't reduce our potential; it should certainly not reduce the effort that we put forward or our belief in ourselves. We must learn from the bad cycles and focus on the good cycles to avoid failure.

Success will broaden your life and lead to even greater success. Once we have experienced success in one area of life, it will give us more confidence in other areas. This will lead to greater success in those areas with less time and effort required to achieve it.

We'll discuss each one of these steps in more detail in the following chapters.

Rocks to Diamonds Cycle

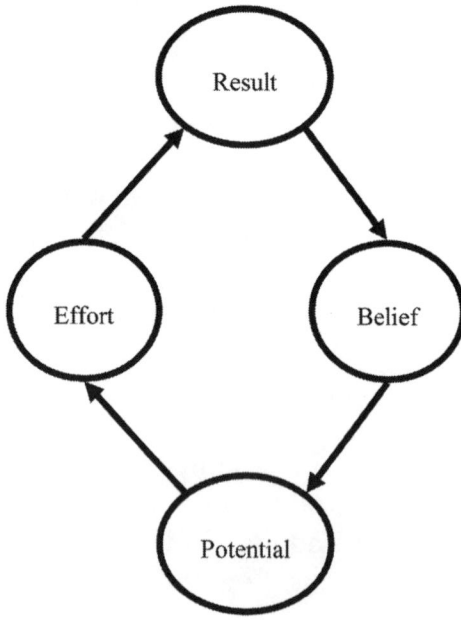

Summary

When we take one hour a day and apply ourselves to learning something new, we can use this *Rocks to Diamonds Cycle* to master what we're learning. The repetition leads to improvement. Some times the improvement may be small but over time the consistency of our effort will yield great results.

We can apply this *Rocks to Diamonds* method to almost any area of our lives. However, this cycle applies to situations where there are a series of steps or loops involved. It would not apply to a one-time only event, such as a lawsuit or winning the lottery.

Chapter 8: Rocks = Our Potential

Personal Growth Is a Joy of a Lifetime

More Potential Than Imaginable

I honestly believe that we miss so much in life because we don't understand the incredible potential we possess. To help you see your potential more clearly, review the following questions:

How do you see yourself?
- Worthless
- Not able to succeed
- Lacking potential
- **Created by God**
- **Designed to be great**
- **Put on earth for a unique purpose**

How do you spend your time?
- Working
- Watching television
- Existing
- **Enjoying every incredible day**
- **Loving the people in your life**
- **Experiencing God's creation**

How do you view other people?
- Boring
- Threatening
- A way to get what I want
- **An opportunity to learn more**
- **An amazing heart**
- **A thrill to be around**

How do you perceive the world around you?
- It's nice
- The weather is okay
- I wish I lived somewhere else
- **Amazed at the beauty of each day**
- **Thrilled to be able to take a walk and enjoy the wonders of nature**
- **Inquisitive about how each part of creation fits together in such an awesome manner**

Do you have any idea what your potential might be? I would say that no one knows his or her true potential because it's limitless. It's fun to learn about our potential. This is one of the reasons why I recommend that we set goals. Our periodic review of our goals will show us our progress toward realizing our potential. We often start out in life with a limited view of what we can do. All too often, we base what we can do on what we've done in the past, but that will always be less than what we're capable of doing. We truly have unlimited potential locked up inside of us, so if we use it, we can truly do almost anything that we want to do.

Do you know what a geode is? It is a rock that looks plain on the outside but has a beautiful crystalline interior. If we saw a pile of geodes, we probably wouldn't give them any special regard because they look like plain rocks. However, if we cut one open, we'd find beauty on the inside.

We are like geodes: from the outside, we may appear plain, but once we look inside, we find that we are filled with a treasure of gifts and talents. Everyone is truly beautiful on the inside.

Chapter 8: Rocks = Our Potential

We really don't have any idea of our true potential. I remember being told that I would never make it in university by my high school teachers and counselors who knew me, or thought they knew me. What they saw was a troubled young man who had attitude problems. What they didn't see was that I had a lot of drive and ambition. Without channels for that drive and ambition, I was bored and frustrated. But when I got a chance to use them later in life, I came alive and accomplished what I feel are great things. I still believe that the best is yet to come in my life.

Our potential is truly unlimited. We must find ways to use the potential we possess. Try new things all the time. Experiment with what we think we would like to do. Don't just blindly follow what others tell us to do. Often they're talking from their limited experience with us, so they don't know what we could achieve if we were given the opportunity. No matter what we want to do, a whole tribe of people will tell us that we can't do it or that it can't be done. If we listen to them, we may find ourselves not succeeding.

When I was a teenager, I wanted to move to California. I was told that it was impossible to get to California from Nova Scotia - not physically impossible, but impossible for someone like me who was performing at less than my potential. This would have been terribly limiting had I truly believed it. However, two people showed me that this wasn't true.

The first one was Denny Doherty, a member of the popular musical group *The Mamas and the Papas,* who was from Halifax. Not only had he made it to California, but he was also a member of one of the great groups of that time. The second happened when I was in grade nine. My homeroom teacher left during the school year to go to California to get married. Despite the fact that people had said it was impossible to get from Nova Scotia to California, here were two people who contradicted that idea and allowed me to have hope of going there.

When I was thirty years old, I moved to California and lived there for the next twenty-five years. So much for being impossible!

Until the sixteenth century, people believed that the earth was the center of the solar system until Copernicus wrote that the sun was the center of our solar system.

Christopher Columbus set sail on his remarkable voyage to find a westward passage to the East. It is worth noting that Columbus was a failure in that he did not do what he set out to do, yet he is regarded as one of the great men in the history of the world. Why did he achieve success? Because he set out to do something! He had a goal and took action to achieve it.

Many people believed that heavier-than-air flight was impossible until the Wright brothers did it.

A large number of people believed that a man of color could not get elected president of the United States until Barack Obama went out and did it.

We can look at history and see case after case of people going against the grain and achieving great success. We all have great potential within us; we just have to find a way to tap into it to achieve our goals.

Not everyone has the same potential. God gives each of us a unique set of gifts and talents that we need for our specific purpose. It is necessary for us to find out what that special purpose is and to go after it.

Gifts and Talents

When we were born, we already possessed our gifts and talents. Unfortunately, we must find out for ourselves what those gifts and talents are to be truly happy. I believe that we can find contentment in a career by using one of these skills, but we won't realize our full potential for joy and happiness until we discover what our real gifts and talents are and develop them.

We will be successful when we're doing what we were designed to do. That means that it is important that we discover our gifts and talents and then develop them.

I was very lucky because God told me as a little boy that I was to be a teacher, giving me a sense of purpose in life. I never doubted that it would happen or that I would be able to do it. Even though in my twenties I knew nothing I could teach anyone and was so introverted that I couldn't talk to two people without getting flustered, I persevered. Just like magic, the doors in life opened to me and finally led me to be a professor at age twenty-nine. The first time I stepped into a classroom, I loved it and had that feeling of being off in another world. By being persistent, I was ready when the opportunities presented themselves.

During my career, I was often offered better paying jobs with more prestige, but I never for one minute considered accepting any of them. I was doing what I was designed to do, so it would have been foolish to change my career. If we are truly happy with our job, it is probably not because of the money but because we are utilizing our gifts and talents. Conversely, if we are unhappy with our job, it is probably not because of the money but because we are not able to fully use our gifts and talents.

There is an old saying, "*Choose a job you love and you will never have to work a day in your life.*"

Life Experiences

We learn not only from formal education but also from life experiences. What we learn from life can be positive or negative, depending on what experiences we have. We may have learned lessons that were completely compatible with our gifts and talents. These experiences helped us develop them and prepared us for using them. On the other hand, our life experiences may have blocked our gifts and talents. These may have actually prevented us from discovering and developing them.

Parents are a great influence on us. As our primary caregivers for the first part of our lives, what they teach us is very significant and will last a lifetime for many people. If we had loving parents, then we likely developed a strong sense of self-worth. If they exposed us to many different sports, hobbies, activities, and educational experiences, then we had a greater chance of discovering what our gifts and talents were at a young age. These positive life experiences make it easier for us to realize our potential.

However, if our parents were ill equipped to be parents, then our life experiences may not have been so encouraging. If our parents were unable to love us because of their own unfortunate dysfunction, then our parents would not have been able to give us a strong sense of self-worth. In fact, the opposite may have happened: they may have given us a weak sense of self-worth, which would make achieving any success more difficult. If they weren't effective parents, then we may have a hard time discovering and developing our gifts and talents.

But the picture is not all bleak for those of us who didn't have the Super Parents. I believe my parents' poor parenting is a major source of my strength today. My father was seldom sober, and my mother was so preoccupied with him that I ended up being neglected as a child. I was often told to do something but given no parental help or supervision. I learned to be very resourceful and to do things by myself. I have a great sense of self-discipline that I feel developed because of the situation at home.

I also learned to be independent, which meant that I could survive adversity and be confident that I would make it. As an adult, I went through divorce and emigration to another country with no family support of any kind. Also, my situation at home motivated me to become successful so I wouldn't end up like my dad. (I feel that my dad wasted his life through his excessive use of alcohol.) That meant getting an education, which has made all the difference in my life. The motivational speaker, Wayne Dyer, says a similar thing happened to him. His father's abandonment of the family led him to learn self-reliance. That is a major theme of his philosophy of life.

Individuals with great parents can turn out to be unsuccessful in life. On the other hand, many people who had bad childhoods and seem to have everything going against them can become hugely successful in life. *It is not our situation that determines our success as much as our response to the situation.*

If we look at two people who grew up in the same bad environment, we might see that they had very different responses to the situation. One responds by refusing to let the hardships hurt. He becomes determined to succeed in life. The other person growing up in the same household gives up and becomes an alcoholic, feeling sorry for himself because of what happened during his childhood.

We must never live in the past!

We must never live in the future!

We must only live in the present!

In other words, what happened to us in our past need not control our present. What might or might not happen in the future should not affect what we do today, unless of course, we can predict that our actions will have direct consequences. We shouldn't live today in fear that in the future something bad might happen, such as getting cancer. However, we shouldn't go out and rob a bank today feeling that what happens tomorrow doesn't matter. We must live in the present while keeping in mind that our actions today may affect the future. We must always live in the present because it is the only time when we have any power to make choices and take action.

Discovering Your Unique Talent

A real problem for many people is discovering their true gifts and talents. Often people haven't spent much time trying to figure this out. Usually we are so busy going and doing in today's society that we don't stop and contemplate. In this age of electronics, people are often involved with some form of communication or entertainment device. Many people just don't take the time to think.

While driving in the car, we have time to contemplate life and our future. When we go for a walk or exercise we have time to use our minds for reflection. Every day there are opportunities to think about the purpose of our time spent here on earth.

Discovering our talents requires that we take some time to stop and contemplate our lives. Doing so may mean reading books and doing some exercises to determine what our gifts are. Whatever method we use, we need to take definite action toward discovering our gifts and talents.

One approach is to think of what has made us extremely happy in the past. Another is to talk to family members, friends, and teachers and ask them what they think our gifts and talents might be. A third method is to review what types of work we have done and see what we were very good at.

Unfortunately, there is no easy answer to finding our gifts and talents. The two methods that I would recommend above all the others are prayer and meditation. Your subconscious mind or your Spirit may have the answer. If you pray, you are asking your Spirit what you want to know. At the same time your subconscious mind picks up what you are looking for. When you meditate you are listening to your subconscious mind and your Spirit. We should pray and meditate until we receive the answer.

Meaning and Purpose in Life

Sometimes we find meaning and purpose from unusual circumstances. If we are open and seeking them, we will find them. I once had a student who was doing okay with her studies but never knew where she was going for a career. During her junior year, her grandmother in Virginia had a bad fall and suffered serious injuries. Since she was close to her grandmother and since no one else in the family was able to go to the grandmother's home to help her, my student decided to take time from her studies and help her grandmother.

She spent three months nursing her grandmother back to health. When she returned to school, she came to see me and tell me that she was changing her major. I hardly recognized her because she had changed from a low energy, unmotivated person into a very energetic, highly motivated person. She said that the time with her grandmother had shown her what her true purpose was, and she decided to switch her major from business to nursing. The last time I heard from her, she was happily involved in a career in nursing.

When people want to determine what their purpose is in life, we often think that their life lacks meaning. They want to find a purpose that will give them a sense of significance. However, we can't find our sense of purpose until we have determined what our gifts and talents are. *Purpose in life is simply using our gifts and talents as they were meant to be used.*

My gift is teaching. When I talk in front of a group, such as at Toastmasters, I feel completely content and in my element. I feel that this is what I should be doing. I guess you could say that this is when I feel closest to God because I know that I'm doing exactly what He designed me to do.

It may be difficult and it may take some time, but when we find the thing that we were designed to do, our whole life shifts and we'll have more inner joy and peace. No one has to tell us when that happens. We will know before anyone else does.

I believe that the two greatest days in our lives are the day we were born and the day we discovered why!

Personal Growth Exercise:

What are your gifts and talents in life?
What special skills were you born with?
What interests do you have?
What abilities do you have?
What are you good at?

Stop and complete this written exercise before going on!

Be part of the successful 2 percent and complete the exercise now!

Summary

It would be interesting if there was a way to measure our potential. We would be truly amazed at what we could do. Since there is no way to measure exactly what our potential is, we must work throughout our lives assuming that we are not reaching the limits of our potential.

Our potential is our gifts and talents. These were inside us when we were born. The problem is that no one ever tells us what they are. We must find them for ourselves and that can be a life long process. Often we think we have discovered our gifts and talents but we are only part way there. I believe that we could always be expanding the use of our gifts and talents our whole lives.

Once we have found our gifts and talents and start to use them and develop them, then our life will take on meaning and a sense of purpose. This is the source of happiness.

Chapter 9: Effort = Using Our Potential

Effort is your choice

The Legacy of Buddy Holly

Why is it that some people apply so much effort to what they do? I visited the Buddy Holly museum in Lubbock, Texas and was amazed by how much influence he had on other performers. Although you may not know who Buddy Holly was, you probably have seen and heard the results of his influence. Buddy Holly died in a plane crash on February 3, 1959, at the age of twenty-two. During his short life, he was a dedicated musician. At the age of twelve he discovered a talent for playing the guitar. He was completely absorbed with playing and writing music and promoting rock 'n' roll.

He spent virtually every minute of every day on his music. The effort he put into music wasn't hardship or work, for he did it for the love of music. He applied his effort completely to his music.

Who was influenced by his efforts?
- He established the model for rock 'n' roll bands that has been used for the past fifty years
- The first forty songs by the Beatles were heavily influenced by his work

- The Rolling Stones, the Hollies, Peter and Gordon, and many other groups of the 1960s were influenced by him
- Elton John, who is famous for wearing outlandish eyeglasses, first wore them to imitate Buddy Holly

If we apply effort to our potential, we will have an influence way beyond anything that we can imagine. As we see with Buddy Holly, we don't have to have a long career to influence people.

Applying Effort Is Your Choice

I wasted my teenage years because I was filled with bitterness and resentment. For years I told myself that it wasn't my fault. I believed it was my dad's fault and that I was just an innocent bystander. But I've come to realize that my response to my home life was *my* responsibility. I chose to feel the way I did. That was a difficult truth to accept.

As I've mentioned before, I grew up in a dysfunctional home with an alcoholic father and a mother who was distracted by my dad's drinking. "Poor me, no one loves me" was my attitude in childhood, and it carried over into my adulthood also.

Out of that experience grew bitterness, and out of bitterness grew resentment. When I first started my personal growth, I looked back and realized that I never worried about the future. I wasn't afraid of life. I didn't have many of the fears that I saw in people around me. Instead, the predominant emotion of my life had been resentment toward my parents. During my teenage years, because of the pain I felt, I experienced two conflicting options for the future: one was running away and the other was suicide. Fortunately, I did not do either one.

Someone with this attitude doesn't experience life positively. My bad attitude led me to not apply myself at school and to withdraw from friends and family and to develop bad habits. I wasn't a discipline problem and rebellious, but I was the opposite - I withdrew from life and tried to be invisible.

Chapter 9: Effort = Using Our Potential

This affected my development. I basically stopped growing emotionally at age fourteen and didn't start again until I started therapy. Please don't be like me and waste a portion of your life. It's important that we not waste one single day, one single hour, or one single minute living in the past because no matter how hard we try, *we cannot change our past.*

One of the big breakthroughs in my therapy was forgiving my parents. I was living in the past by holding on to the anger and resentment that I felt for my parent's dysfunctional behavior. I could never focus on the current events in my life because I was always stuck in the past. However, once I forgave my parents, I was freed from the past and was able to live more in the present moment. It was a huge change in my life.

How can we forgive someone? I worked at it in therapy and prayer. One day I suddenly saw the situation differently. Instead of focusing on me and my pain, I focused on my parents and their pain. Like me, they grew up in dysfunctional homes and were doing the best job that they could. Their bad parenting wasn't malicious, just a product of their own childhoods. This made forgiving them much easier. Forgiving is truly freeing.

The only time in which we have any power is the present. We can't change the past or what we experienced. We can't live in the future because it is not guaranteed to anyone. We can only live in the present.

We need to live today to the maximum. We must completely apply ourselves to everything we do. When I get up in the morning, I often exercise first thing while listening to a motivational CD. I'm fully present and experience my exercise as exhilarating. It sets a great tone for the day. When I run, I love the time. I enjoy feeling the strain, managing my breathing, watching the sky and the weather, and just being alone in God's wonderful creation.

Every morning I do devotionals that include reading my Bible, reading inspirational materials, and praying about my day and what's going on in my life.

Whatever I do during the day, whether it is work, volunteering, spending time with friends, or hiking in nature, I try to be

100 percent present and aware of my life every minute. I don't want to waste one more day of my life with a bad attitude.

Despite how we may feel, life on earth is short so we must learn to live every moment to the fullest.

Goals

Goals are an important part of effort. They will determine what effort we give, when we give it, and how we give it. Our effort is much more effective if we focus it on a single goal or a small group of goals. Let's look at the sun's rays as an example. Sunlight hits the surface of the earth and warms it. If we take that sunlight and focus it through a magnifying glass, that same sunlight will start a fire.

We can apply effort to carry out our potential for a certain effect. But, as with the magnifying glass, if we focus that effort on our goals, we'll magnify our power and achieve much greater results. *By focusing our effort on the proper goals, we'll progress more rapidly and achieve results beyond our expectations.*

Motivation

Let's do an exercise about motivation. Let's pretend to go for a nice walk. Take a few minutes and close your eyes and take a walk with me. Please stop reading and do this exercise for two minutes.

STOP! Stop reading and take a walk in your mind!

When you finish your walk, go to the next page.

Think about and write down what went through your mind on your imaginary walk.

Were you wondering:

Where am I supposed to be?
Where am I supposed to be going?
How long am I supposed to walk?
What am I supposed to be doing as I walk?

Most people like structure in their lives. They want to know where they're going, how long it'll take to get there, and why they're going somewhere. Unfortunately, having these answers may lead to two problems:

1. We may think only in the short term, as it is easier to achieve the certainty that we crave.
2. We may listen to what others tell us about how to lead our lives.

Since many people don't know how to plan their own lives (after all, when were they taught that?), they don't have a plan and are all too willing to live without long-term goals or to accept what someone else tells them. Notice that the questions that I thought you might have during the imaginary walk all contained "supposed to." This implies we desired someone to tell us what to do instead of figuring it out for ourselves.

There is a great scene in the movie *The Dead Poets Society* when the professor takes the students to an outdoor plaza and tells them to walk around; he gives them no other rules or directions. At first everyone is bewildered that they have been told to do something without specific directions and they're tentative about walking. But slowly, each person starts doing something different. This feels uncomfortable for many students, and they start following the patterns of others rather than their inner selves.

When my students asked me which careers they should choose, I often got the feeling that they didn't want my opinion to throw in with the other opinions to ponder. Instead, I felt they wanted me to tell them which career to choose and the five steps to get there.

Fortunately for them, I didn't give them specific answers. I probed to find out what they wanted to do and what they were good at. I asked them what they dreamed of doing if there were no limits in life. Then I would encourage them to follow their dreams even if they thought it was impossible or unlikely that they could.

A plan is a wonderful motivator. For example, my plan was to write this book. As I wrote, I became completely focused on it. When I read or talked to people, my mind always related ideas back to the book:

That is a great point! Where could I use it?
That could be a chapter title!
That is a great quote!
I could incorporate that idea into my book.

I taught public speaking because I think that the ability to speak in public is important to success. If I gave my students specific directions, they moaned and groaned but accepted them and asked very few questions. However, if I gave them an assignment for a three-minute speech with no guidelines or no rules to follow, the questions came fast and furious. It wasn't unusual for a student to approach me on campus outside of class with a question.

It's human nature to want a certain degree of structure. We are wired that way. That's one reason we can accomplish more by having goals: they provide us with structure.

We need to make *our own* plan. We should spend time setting goals as discussed earlier. We must make our own goals and not just accept what someone else tells us. Setting goals may take some time and effort, but it will pay off in the long run. A life lived with purpose will give us a life of significance, and we will enjoy living much more.

Chapter 9: Effort = Using Our Potential

Time

The two most important elements to manage are cash and time, with time being the most important by far. There are two reasons why:

1. We have a limited amount of time. No matter what we do, there is no way to extend the amount of time we have in our lives.
2. There is unlimited cash available for us to use. A good idea will attract cash.

We live in a world where people seem to be in such a hurry to get where they're going that they don't really stop and think about where they're going or why.

Just think of dating and marriage. Many people are so anxious to get married that they rush through the dating process and don't really enjoy the magic of getting to know the other person. Dating should be like a long slow dance. Too often people rush through the dating stage to get to the wedding but then end up divorced because they didn't lay the proper foundation in the dating stage.

I know that you may be thinking about an apparent contradiction in this idea. How can we live in the present but work toward our goals in the future? When I say live in the present, I mean that we want to appreciate and do our best in every moment. We don't want to be absorbed with what happened in the past or worried about what will happen in the future. We want our minds to be present at all times. By working toward our goals we are living in the present but working to make the future wonderful also.

Happiness or success happens when we're absorbed in working toward our goals. That means living in the present but also planning for and doing other work that will benefit our future. The great American writer, Edith Wharton, said that *"If only we'd stop trying to be happy, we could have a pretty good time."* This means that if we're only focused on our happiness, we'll have trouble being happy. Also, if we chase happiness itself, we too often take shortcuts such as using drugs and alcohol that prove not to work in the long term. Instead, happiness is a by-product of pursuing our goals.

I have observed that people who are busy with life are often happier than those who are looking for happiness. For example, I have seen friends who don't think about happiness, they just get absorbed in their work and are happy doing it. They're not looking for happiness; it just happens as a by-product of their work. On the other hand, I pursued happiness in my life. I was very aware of how unhappy I was. Instead of seeking happiness, we need to pursue our goals using our God-given gifts. Happiness will result as a by-product.

We always need to keep our goals in mind and work toward them in the present. If we don't work toward our goals, our next present moments may not be so enjoyable.

We can live in the present but completely ignore the future, for example, if we commit a crime. A criminal will do something wrong today completely ignoring the fact that he might get caught and have to face the consequences of his action.

Most people don't commit crimes because they realize that there will be consequences in the future. Crime is an example of living in the present but harming the future. Instead, *our actions in the present must be consistent with our goals for the future.*

Types of Effort

The three types of effort are:
Physical
Mental
Spiritual

The body, mind, and Spirit also give us the three types of effort that we can use. The effort we use will vary depending on the situation. But there is seldom a situation that requires a single type of effort. We usually need a balance of the three.

Let's look at an example. When we study for a big exam, what type of effort do we use? Mental effort! But we don't use mental effort alone. We'll be much more successful if we incorporate physical effort to stimulate our minds, reduce stress, stay awake when studying, and sleep better the night before the exam. We must also include Spiritual effort for the motivation to succeed and the belief that we are worthy of the success.

The three types of effort are in a hierarchy of power. Physical effort is the most limited, and used alone, it will yield the most limited results. However, mental effort is almost unlimited and will multiply our physical effort and therefore the results that we achieve. Spiritual energy is beyond anything that we can imagine. If we engage Spiritual effort, hold on, because we'll probably go places and do things that we never dreamed were possible.

Let's see how this applies to a simple activity like picking up a heavy object. If we exert only physical effort, we'll simply bend over and pick the object up, or try to pick it up. This may work fine, but it may not work if the object is too heavy for us.

If we are having trouble lifting the heavy object, we could apply some mental effort and think, "How else could I do this to get a better result?" The answer will come if we give ourselves a few minutes to engage our minds and tap into our subconscious. The solution may be as simple as using a lever or pulley or it may be more complicated. No matter what the solution, a little thought as to how to do it better will make picking up the object much easier.

Finally, if we apply Spiritual effort, we are almost unlimited in what we can do. Think of a story about a mother who picks up a car that has fallen on her child when normally she wouldn't have the physical strength. She doesn't have time to use mental effort; she has to act immediately. She is just so motivated by the thought of her child being crushed by the car that she does an amazing act. There is only one explanation for her strength: she uses Spiritual effort to accomplish this amazing feat.

We need to use all three types of effort in every situation. Using all three together will make the process easier and will allow us to accomplish much more.

I firmly believe that we humans limit what we think we can achieve. We shortchange ourselves when we limit our thinking or use negative thinking and say, "I can't."

I remember a time when I talked to a student about this. She doubted what I said was true. I told her she could do almost anything that she wanted to do, but she told me that the idea was stupid. She exclaimed with some delight (since she thought that she had proved me wrong), "Well, I can't fly!" I pointed out to her that there were several airports in the Bay Area from which she could fly anywhere in the world if she wanted. *We can accomplish almost anything, but sometimes we must shift the way we think.*

This is an example of the limits we place upon ourselves. Too often, we immediately think of what we can't do. I've told other people they can do almost anything, and they have a similar response to my student. They'll try to think of the *one* situation in which they can't do it, and so they won't try. If we say that we can't do something, we have certainty in our world. However, if we suspend these thoughts and think of the possibility of doing it, then we have uncertainty, which is very uncomfortable for many people. I know that there have been circumstances in my life when I made bad decisions. Afterward, I wondered why I had done something that was against what I believed. Often it was because I couldn't stand the uncertainty of the moment. I decided in favor of the choice that gave me certainty and not the choice that gave me the best result.

One of the worst examples was an investment I made. I had saved up some money and wanted to invest it in a business. After I started searching for an investment, I got anxious because I found so many businesses to buy, but I didn't know much about most of them. My anxiety caused me to proceed too quickly and invest in a business that I knew nothing about. I lost all my money within a year. If I hadn't been so anxious and taken my time, I probably would have realized that investing in a business wasn't the best thing for me at that time.

We need to think the opposite way in this area. Instead of looking for the one example where what we want to do won't work, we need to look for the one example where it can work. Once we see the one way it can work, then we will see even more possibilities. This is a powerful tool. If we look at Roger Bannister, the first person to run a mile in less than four minutes, we see a fine example. Until 1954 when he broke the record, it was believed that it was impossible for a human to run a mile in less than four minutes. But Bannister ran just over the four minute mark and believed that with more training he could break the record. That is exactly what he did because he believed that he could.

Here is the important lesson. The year after he ran the sub four minute mile, dozens of other runners did it also. As soon as people believed that it was possible, they were able to do it also. The only thing that had changed was their belief about the four minute mile.

It seems that once we get thinking in one direction we just continue in that way. This thinking is like being on railway tracks in that once we start on them we can only go where they go. This can be in the right or wrong direction as seen in the following spirals:

Spiral 1:

Positive thinking breeds success!
Success breeds more success!
Success breeds positive thinking!
Positive thinking breeds success!

Spiral 2:

Negative thinking breeds failure!
Failure breeds more failure!
Failure breeds negative thinking!
Negative thinking breeds failure!

One of these spirals goes up and the other goes down. Which one should we choose? That choice is completely up to us and no one else in the world. After all, we control our thoughts.

Compare the world today to the world of one hundred years ago. Many people of that day would have said that the computers, cars, planes, phones, televisions, and other forms of technology that we take for granted today would have been impossible. If everyone believed that, they would never have gone out and discovered or developed all these amazing inventions. *Without belief in success, we cannot venture into the unknown.*

Our beliefs about what we can and cannot do are an important part of our effort to succeed. This belief will determine the effort we put forth.

Personal Growth Exercise:

Think of a time when you had to complete a difficult task. What kind of effort did you apply to complete the task?

Think of a time when you had to complete an easy task. What kind of effort did you apply to complete the task?

Describe a creative activity in which you were so wrapped up that you lost all track of time.

How did you feel?

Describe a routine activity that you thought was boring and you didn't really want to do but had to anyway.

How did you feel?

Stop and complete this written exercise before going on!

Chapter 9: Effort = Using Our Potential

Be part of the successful 2 percent and complete the exercise now!

Summary

We get to choose which effort to use every time we do something. If we make poor choices or apply too little effort, we get a poor result. However, if we choose to do our best and use all three types of effort - mind, body, and Spirit - the results are often surprising.

Looking to others is a great way to see what applying effort can do. Buddy Holly is only one individual who has inspired me by showing me what one person can do during a short period of time if he is truly committed to his purpose in life.

Motivation is an important part of effort because it points us in the right direction. We can achieve great things in life if we are going in the right direction and are applying our best effort.

Time is an interesting concept to understand. We sometimes feel like we have so much and at other times we feel like we have so little. The truth is we have a limited amount of time on earth. It is important that we use our time wisely. I don't mean that we should be driven madly to achieve our goals but I certainly feel that we should be striving all the time towards them.

Finally, effort can be physical, mental or Spiritual but it is best when it is a balance of the three.

Chapter 10: Result = Benefit of Our Effort

There Is No Greater Reward for a Job Well Done Than the Personal Satisfaction of Having Done It

Vision of Success

Once we have completed our activity, we need to assess the result. It was important that we had a goal or plan before we started so that we know if we have accomplished what we set out to do. This will give us a standard, or benchmark, with which to compare our result.

Some people are lucky and just fall into success. Look at Christopher Columbus. He never achieved his specific goal, yet he became one of the most famous people in history. But usually when we do not achieve our goal, we are not so lucky. Note that Columbus did have a goal and applied lots of effort in trying to achieve it. Success was the by-product of his action to achieve his goal.

It is better to have a high goal and fall short than to have a goal that is too low and achieve it.

The more definite our goal at the beginning, the easier it is to know if we achieved it. For example, let's say that we wanted to be a great doctor, and we scored 60 percent on our exams in medical school and went on to become a doctor. Did we reach our goal? If our goal was simply to be a doctor, then, yes we succeeded. But I doubt anyone would be too eager to go to a doctor who just squeaked in above the pass line (or fail line, depending upon how we look at it) on his or her exams. Many people would feel that we didn't achieve our goal because we haven't become a great doctor. Assessing whether we achieved our goal all depends on how we defined our goal at the beginning. Of course, we can always change that goal as we progress.

The vision that we hold when we start our activity will determine how successful we are once it is complete.

I volunteer at a local theater designing, building, and painting sets for plays. I just love doing it. I enjoy it so much that I get lost in the process and become totally absorbed and happy. In building the sets, the crew's motto is, "We're not building a piano." In other words, we build a set to look nice for seven weeks while the play is running and then be torn down. This of course is opposite to how a piano is made with lots of fabulous craftsmanship so that it plays well for decades. Our vision is a set that looks good, is safe, is strong enough to stay up for seven weeks, and is easy to take down when we're finished with it. I hope that the piano maker's vision would be much different than that.

When we have a very definite vision of what we want to do, the task is easier to do, and we are better able to tell when we're finished. Writing a book like this can be very difficult if we don't manage the process. What does the final book look like? How many pages does it have? How many chapters? It is almost impossible to know in advance what the final product will look like. But, we must have some criteria in order to know when we're finished.

Many people don't write books or paint pictures because they won't know when they have a finished product. Others begin to write a book or paint a picture but never know when they're finished, so they continuously improve it. They might eventually discard their work because they can't identify the finished product. We should always have some way of determining when we're finished or success will elude us.

Chapter 10: Result = Benefit of Our Effort

We need to define what success looks like to us and realize how we'll recognize it when we achieve it. For example, I heard two men talking one day about success. One man was stressed because he came up short of his definition of success. The other man was content and relaxed because he had met his definition of success. I asked them what their definitions were. The man who was stressed was financially successful, but he defined success as earning more than one million dollars a year, and he was a little bit short of that goal. The other man was much less financially successful, but he had defined success as waking up above ground (i.e. still alive). He felt successful every morning before he even got out of bed, and anything he achieved beyond that for the rest of the day was icing on the cake.

We should define our goal as something that is achievable. It should make us stretch in the direction in which we want to go to achieve a greater long term goal. We must not set a goal that is too low because then we'll never realize our true potential. At the same time, we must not set a goal that is unachievable because we'll get frustrated and give up. The two men in the previous example set goals that didn't stretch them toward a long term goal. They both failed to set appropriate goals.

The *Rocks to Diamonds Cycle* has discrete steps as we go through each loop, so we should remember to create steps toward our goals. Each step should be achievable to build confidence and spur us on toward greater success. For example, if we want to learn something like sailing, we don't set a goal of being a captain after the first time out, even though being a captain is our long-term goal. Along the way, we set a goal of learning how to trim the sails. Then we set a higher goal of learning the points of sail. We keep raising the bar. By using this step method, we grow into our vision.

Persistence and Perseverance

One of the greatest determining factors of success is persistence or perseverance. Many people quit close to reaching their goals because they lose heart, stop believing, and give up. The person who has her heart set on a vision and won't give up until she achieves it will almost always be successful. The person who quits is by definition not successful.

Singers and musicians are often said to be an "overnight success." People envy them because they seem to have gone from nothing to being hugely successful. But if we looked at the performers' past, we would find years and years of grinding it out, practicing, playing for unappreciative audiences, and not giving up their dream.

I grew up in Nova Scotia, in eastern Canada. It seemed like when I went to a special event, the same girl was always singing. She often was unappreciated by her audience since she wasn't the headliner, but that never seemed to phase her. She just kept on singing and performing. Today that girl, Anne Murray, is a hugely successful international singer. To me she exemplifies how perseverance is rewarded by success. She has been a great inspiration to me because she set such a great example of what a person could achieve through perseverance.

That is not to say that perseverance is always appropriate. Sometimes we have to look at the results of our intermediate steps and ask ourselves if we are going in the right direction. A lack of success can be an indication that we're going down the wrong road. An example might be baseball players who focus solely on becoming professionals and then end up wasting many good years in dead-end attempts to get to the big time. There's a big difference between quitting and changing your goals along the way.

We must also balance what we're chasing with the cost of achieving it. As a youth I dreamed of being a politician and making a social contribution. However, I worked for a man who was a politician and saw the price he paid in his family life. After carefully assessing the pros and cons, I decided not to pursue that dream. The price was just too high for me. As it turned out, my choice allowed me to get into the absolutely right career, as a professor teaching accounting and computers.

Chapter 10: Result = Benefit of Our Effort

Where Do You Want to Go from Here?

Once we have achieved a goal, we must set the next goal. Do we want to continue to reach higher in the same direction? Do we want to change direction? Seldom does someone start on a long journey and complete it without changing course along the way.

When I was a young man, I saw that education was the way out of the dysfunctional home in which I had been raised. I went to university with the idea of becoming an engineer, but physics did me in. Then I took mathematics and chemistry and got my degree in those two subjects. Those subjects still didn't lead me where I wanted to go. But by getting my degree, I was moving in the right direction, as it opened the door for the next much more important step in my career. I went back to school and earned my Chartered Accountancy designation in Canada, and this got me a long way toward where I wanted to go. Later I got an MBA and Certified Public Accountant certification in California, which further helped me along.

My overriding vision was that I would be a teacher. Where? When? Of what? I didn't know when I set out, but each of these steps got me closer to my ultimate goal. How could I tell if I achieved my goal? When I became a professor, I knew that I was doing what God had designed me to do. I never thought about another job or even the same job at another university. Since I felt like California State University in Hayward was exactly where I was supposed to be, I stayed there for twenty-five years even though I had originally planned to stay for just one.

Life will have twists and turns that we won't be able to foresee, but if we keep a vision (even a blurry one) of success in our minds all the time, we will eventually get to the right place. More people who have a vision for their life succeed than those who don't have a vision or a plan or goals of any kind.

Patience

One of our greatest weaknesses today is our lack of patience. It seems that we expect to get what we want right now. But one of the reasons victory can be so sweet is that it takes time to achieve. Just think of how sweet it is to graduate from university after years of hard work and sacrifice. Think about the thrill of winning the World Series after a season of over two hundred games and years of conditioning and practice. Waiting patiently and working toward a goal make success all the more precious when we finally get it.

I feel that our lack of patience is what has gotten us into the huge financial crisis that we're experiencing. I am afraid that we are missing the real lesson to be learned here because we are too busy blaming Wall Street and greed for the problem. The problem is a personal problem that we as individuals have created. We can blame others, but we must accept our share of the responsibility.

Up to the 1960's banks offered very little credit, and it was very difficult to obtain. Just think of a world with no credit cards or lines of credit. Believe it or not, people actually used cash!

If we wanted something, we saved up our money until we could pay cash for it. Under these circumstances, people tended to make wiser decisions. One time a friend asked my advice about purchasing a car. She wondered what she should buy. I asked her how much money she had saved up for a car, and she said she had $5,000. I told her to buy a $5,000 car. She ignored my advice and bought the car she wanted instead of the car she could afford.

Let's say we want to buy a car but no credit is available. We might save for two years and finally have $5,000. During those two years, we would most likely have been dreaming about getting our car. We would have been researching and test-driving the various cars that we could purchase. We would probably take lots of time to shop around to get the best car for $5,000. Once we purchased it, we would be extremely happy because we worked toward this goal for more than two years and made a financially sound decision.

However, this is not the way we do things today. Now we start by shopping for cars until we find the one we like, not the one we can afford or that fits our needs. Then we buy it using borrowed money. The more expensive the car, the greater the depreciation and the greater the interest we'll have to pay on our loan. Sometimes the cost of insurance on a new car is also dramatically higher than on a used car.

The thing that people fail to see here is that if we had bought a $5,000 car with our savings, we'd have *no* monthly payments to make. We'd be free to spend or save our paychecks as we please. However, if we buy a car with borrowed money, we must repay that money with interest. This means that we've spent part of our subsequent paychecks before we've even earned them. *When we buy on credit, we give away our future.*

Living a debt-free life is incredible. It may mean not having new cars or fancy toys, but it means having true freedom. When we get paid, we can do what we want with our money. There are many other benefits to debt-free living: no commitment to a bank, better sleep, lack of worry about making future payments, and fewer arguments with our spouse or partner. One of the most common arguments couples have is about money. Debt-free living eliminates this stress.

There are a lot of benefits to patience and a lot of drawbacks to impatience. When going after a goal, we need to be patient with ourselves and with the process but never stop pursuing it. Any goal that we hold for a long time and work diligently toward is more likely to be the right goal for us. We will appreciate it all the more once we achieve it.

If we're patient, we're more likely to be chasing the right goal because we have time to evaluate our goal along the way. Many people who buy cars on credit regret it later because they didn't take the time to consider what was right for them and work toward the goal. Fewer people who save up regret their purchases because as they saved, they had time to assess their choice and research their options.

I believe that patience is a great virtue, and the practice of patience will increase the quality of our lives and happiness immensely.

We must work toward our goals, and when we do not achieve them, we must not be disheartened. We must continue to learn from our past and improve our future. Do we need to modify our goal or continue to pursue it? Eventually we will reach our chosen goal. It is a wonderful day when we have reached a long sought-after goal.

Personal Growth Exercise:

Successful people can be divided into two groups:

1) Process-oriented people who care more about the process than the result. If such a person were to play tennis, he would enjoy the act of playing and not focus on the score at the end.
2) Results-oriented people who live for the result and don't care that much about the process. This type of person would focus on the score of a tennis match rather than who played best or who had the most fun.

Which kind of person are you? It is important to know your style when you make major decisions. For example, I am a results oriented person and I am currently looking at homes to purchase. I don't enjoy the process and I get frustrated that it takes so long to find the right house. A process oriented person might enjoy the time of looking and seeing all the different houses available.

How does your style benefit you?

How does your style hurt you?

Stop and complete this written exercise before going on!

Be part of the successful 2 percent and complete the exercise now!

Summary

Our efforts will get us closer to our stated goals. Keeping our long-term vision in mind will help us to work toward short-term goals, as they are simply steps along the way toward the long-term vision for our lives.

Two personal characteristics that will help us achieve goals are persistence and patience. If we do not possess these traits, we can develop them. They will keep us focused on our goals and keep us going when we seem to make little progress or encounter setbacks. Remember the saying of that great football coach Vince Lombardi, "*Winners never quit and quitters never win.*"

We need to be diligent in setting long term goals. As we work toward our short term goals we must always keep in mind our long term goals. This will mean that we will always have a goal to aim at and not suffer let down after we have achieved a goal.

Chapter 11: Belief = Changed by Result

Wealth is the Ability to Fully Experience Life
Thoreau

Feedback Loop

Every good system has a feedback loop that links the end of the process back to the beginning. For example, let's look at manufacturing cars. We have an inspection team at the end that tests the cars. They must communicate the findings to the people building the cars so the builders can improve the quality of the cars they build in the future.

In the *Rocks to Diamonds Cycle*, the feedback connection is critical for believing in ourselves. If we complete the first loop successfully, we have increased confidence going into the second loop. However, if we were unsuccessful at the end of the first loop, we'll have decreased confidence and have a harder time being successful in the second loop.

In my life, the first time the results part of the feedback loop was significant was in junior high school. Depending upon how students did in grade seven, they were grouped going into grade eight. Since I did well in grade seven (this is hard for me to believe, but apparently it was so), in grade eight, I went into grade 8A—the class with all the smart kids. Other students went into 8B, 8C, 8D, 8E, 8F, or 8G. Each subsequent letter indicated that you were a little lower on the academic food chain.

Even though we never knew it, grade seven (unlike any previous grade) decided our fate for the remainder of junior high school and high school. We were labeled and set on a path. Getting put into grade 8A was a great benefit for me. It has made a huge difference in my life. It is amazing that an educator's decision for a thirteen-year-old boy could so significantly set the path for his future.

I never doubted that I could achieve academically, even though my attitude almost sank my boat when I got into high school. During my elementary school years, my teachers saw me as someone who had great potential. I didn't see that and always hated their comments on my report cards that I was not working to my potential. However, that stayed with me and gave me some confidence during my troubled years in high school.

Today, I realize that their reinforcement of the idea that I had great potential got inside me and gave me confidence to go to university and later to undertake my accounting studies. The fact that I was chosen to go to grade 8A was a huge boost to my self-confidence that lasted throughout my life.

Constant feedback from my teachers helped me to see myself in a different light.

Measuring Belief in Yourself

It would be great if we had a device like a bathroom scale that we could use to measure self-confidence. We could measure how much we believed in ourselves at various times along the way to our goal to see if we were improving in self-confidence. That would also help us to determine if we needed to work on our self-confidence in some way.

I know one of the greatest confidence boosts I ever received came completely out of the blue. When I had become an accountant, I dreamed of being a teacher but had low self-confidence. Without self-confidence, I was unable to talk in front of a group of people. This was a major hindrance for a teacher.

Then a man named Ross Towler, a leader in the accounting community in my hometown, contacted me and asked if I would be interested in taking a course at Toastmasters. He explained that it was an organization that helps people become better speakers. The course met one night a week for the next eight weeks.

The first two weeks, I didn't say one word to anyone. Not only did I lack self-confidence, but I discovered that because of my low self-esteem I was terrified of getting up in front of people and talking.

The Toastmasters were patient and encouraging, and the third week, I stood up and said something for the first time. In the eighth week, I was the chairman of the meeting. I had discovered a hidden talent that no one knew was inside of me. Especially me! After that, public speaking became one of my favorite things to do. There are few things in my life that compare to the thrill of talking to a group of people and teaching them something that will improve their lives.

We never know when some event will happen to increase or decrease our self-confidence. It is important to try to monitor our self-confidence and to build it up in whatever way we can. We can build self-confidence by getting an education, by learning a new skill, by losing weight, by giving up a bad habit, or by excelling in a hobby. *Self-confidence comes from success, whether it is big or small, in any area of life.*

Do you have self-confidence or self-consciousness? Self-confidence will improve your performance in every aspect of life. Self-consciousness will hamper your performance and will often prevent you from trying something that could be wonderful. A friend recently expressed this in a different manner. He said that upon entering a room full of people, what do you think? Do you think, "Here I am, I hope someone likes me." (self-consciousness) or, "Here I am, I hope to meet some interesting people." (self-confidence).

Change Belief to Certainty

The greater our self-confidence when beginning something new, the better is our chance of success. But just think if we could raise our confidence to certainty.

Let's look at golf. Many people play golf but lack self-confidence in their skills. Each time they play, they remember all the bad shots they've taken. This can turn what belief they have in themselves to absolute certainty that they're bad at golf. Guess how they play!

But if they began by remembering only the good shots that they made, they would realize that they have the skills to make any shot. Golf consists of three types of shots: long shots, short shots, and putts. On any given day, a player will make a few good shots of each of these types. Those good shots may not be the majority, but that doesn't matter. Even a few is enough to show them that they have the skill to make any shot. Once they believe they can make a shot, they just need to focus on doing it.

Whatever our field of endeavor, we must build our self-confidence. If we strengthen our belief in ourselves until that belief becomes a certainty, we will be much more successful.

A funny thing about confidence is that it spills over into other areas of our lives. If we become confident in one area, we will become more confident overall. The self-confidence a person exudes opens a lot of doors in his or her life.

There is a saying that *"The rich get richer and the poor get poorer."* That really applies to self-confidence. We could say that the people with strong self-confidence get stronger while the people with weak self-confidence get weaker. So we need to work at building up our self-confidence. If we do, we'll see a big improvement in all areas.

Changing Your Belief

When we approach something new, our attitude will often determine the outcome. If we approach something believing that we can master it, then we can. But, if we start by believing that we can't master this new thing, then we won't.

Chapter 11: Belief = Changed by Result

When I taught introductory accounting, it was a required course for all students majoring in business. Many students would enter the class with a terrible attitude that could lead to disaster. It was not unusual to hear a student say, "My friend took this accounting course last year and said that it was the hardest course ever." Or my personal favorite: "I heard that this course is really difficult, so I'll take it this fall and fail and then I'll retake it in the winter and pass." Usually they got the first part of this belief correct. How could they succeed when they began with this attitude?

I spent time the first day of class each quarter trying to change this belief. I heard the same things when I first started to study accounting, but that just motivated me to study harder. I found the tests weren't so difficult, and my grades reflected my hard work. Many students' grades reflected their fears instead.

Students in my classes were required to do lots of homework. An important aspect of learning accounting is doing the homework. This not only helps them learn the material, but it also builds confidence in their ability to do the work. This is an example of the *Rocks to Diamonds Cycle*.

I tried to make all my tests and exams a fair reflection of what I taught in class. To measure each class's performance, I used statistics and expected to see a bell curve, with most grades concentrated around a certain point. For example, let's say that the median grade was 70 percent. We'd then find lots of students with scores between 60 and 80 percent and fewer students with grades in the 50s and 80s and even fewer below 50 or over 90.

But, in accounting classes, the grades typically formed two bell curves instead of one. One bell curve was centered on 75 percent and the other on 40 percent. What caused the difference? It was simply the amount of effort the students put into the course. One group studied and did their homework while the other group didn't.

What many students also discovered was that when they applied themselves to the material in the accounting course, it wasn't as hard as they had imagined. When they did the assigned homework problems, they found they weren't as hard as the students thought they'd be. Each homework problem that they completed successfully raised their level of belief in themselves and their ability to do accounting. This was the *Rocks to Diamond Cycle* in action. Each time they completed a cycle, their self-confidence rose higher. Some got to the point of certainty and earned A grades on exams, and some even went on to become accountants.

Did this success affect other parts of their lives? Since they could handle what they had perceived as one of the most difficult courses in their degree program, this increased their self-confidence in other courses and also in other areas of life. Success breeds more success because it increases our self-confidence.

We need to use this concept to our advantage in life. Whatever we do, we should do our best at it. Afterward, we should be aware of how well we did and let that bolster our self-confidence. Then we can take on bigger challenges. We can take on tasks that we thought were too difficult to prove to ourselves that we can do them. Who knows, we may find our purpose in the process.

Challenge Yourself

> *Accept the Challenges So That You May*
> *Feel the Exhilaration of Victory*
> General George Patton

When I was younger, I did not have the courage to try new things. I played it safe by only doing what I knew I could achieve. If I tried something new, I had low expectations of what I could do and settled for poor results. I wasn't competitive because I had little self-confidence.

I always loved hiking for many reasons such as being outdoors, smelling the fresh air, getting exercise, seeing God's wonderful creation and for me, it was a noncompetitive activity. I could hike as well as or better than my friends because I have long legs and great stamina. Therefore, hiking was a nonthreatening activity.

I went on a weekend backpacking trip that changed my life. I signed up with a hiking group expecting some hiking and overnight camping. This trip took place over Easter weekend, so it lasted three days and two nights. We were to go from Sunol to Del Valle in the San Francisco East Bay.

We started in the morning on Good Friday from Sunol and hiked to our campground for the night. The hike was nothing unusual. We camped out on a cliff overlooking a large canyon. In the middle of the night, I got up and was overcome by the beauty. I can still picture it today as clear as a bell. When I first got out of my tent, I was struck by the bright full moon. I have never seen the moon bigger or brighter than it was that night. I felt like it was closer than normal. Then I walked to the edge of the cliff and was literally overwhelmed with the sight of the canyon.

When I moved to San Francisco, the fog really amazed me. I grew up in a foggy place, and the fog was just there. But in San Francisco, the fog is different: it flows like water in slow motion. I love to watch it flow over a hill or around the city or past the Golden Gate Bridge on its way into the bay.

On this night, the fog flowed into the canyon below and almost filled it. It looked like the canyon was full of white cotton batting. I wanted to jump on top of it and play in it. The full moon shining on the canyon filled with fog was one of the most beautiful sights I have ever seen. It seemed to glow in the moonlight. I didn't attend church at that time, but I didn't doubt that there was a God. How else could there be such beauty in the world?

That evening was just the beginning of the miracles of that weekend. The next day we hiked up and down mountains like there was no end to them. I can remember hiking up one mountain and thinking how difficult it was. I thought that I saw the top just ahead. When I got there, I learned that it wasn't the top but it was just a curve in the trail. This happened over and over until finally I said to myself, "There is no top, only more curves in the trail." Basically I had given up hope of finding the top of the mountain.

That was the second great thing that happened that weekend. I not only learned how to think about hiking in the mountains but also about living life. What I learned was that as I work toward a goal, it's not just around the next curve but instead is somewhere off in the distance. If I keep that distant goal in mind, each curve is just another step closer to the goal. Instead of hiking on an emotional roller coaster, experiencing a high when I expected the top and a low when I discovered it wasn't there, I learned that each segment was just part of the journey. I learned to just enjoy that leg of the journey and then the next leg and the next.

After that weekend I thought about the hike and the fact that I went more than twenty miles while carrying a heavy backpack up and down mountains. If I had known that beforehand, I wouldn't have gone on the trip. But when I looked back on it, what I had thought impossible was only difficult and could be accomplished when it was broken down into small segments. I always knew I could do the next leg, but if that mountain trail had gone straight to the top, I would have quit and believed I couldn't do it.

So it is with life. The path to a goal may seem long and impossible, but when we break it down into small pieces, it is easier to achieve. For example, getting a university degree may sound tough, but when we look at it one semester or one course at a time, it appears doable.

The month after the backpacking trip, I was amazed at what I had accomplished. I started to look for other challenges, not competing against other people, but simply against myself. What else could I accomplish that I thought was impossible for me to do?

I found my next one in riding my bicycle. Riding my bike was always a favorite hobby, but true to my nature, I didn't go on any rides that were too difficult. I lived near Mt. Diablo, which rises to a height of 3,849 feet above sea level and has a lookout on top. The road up was 11 miles long with lots of curves, just like the hike. The elevation gain was over 3,000 feet, which I felt was clearly impossible for a guy like me.

I decided that riding to the lookout on Mt. Diablo was my next challenge. I took my bike to the bottom of the mountain. My goal for the day was to ride to the first gate about three miles up. Then each day I would ride farther until I reached the top. The ride to the first gate wasn't as difficult as I had thought and was actually a lot of fun. Instead of feeling tired when I got there, I felt excited and energized. So I pushed on to the next milestone, which was at six miles. That section was less steep than the first, so it also was not as hard as I had thought. Now I was more than halfway up the mountain and still feeling good. I started the third leg, which was a lot steeper, and after about a mile, I was dead tired. But I was feeling elated because I had done more than I thought possible for me. I didn't make it to the top that day, but I did many times after that, and I felt like a winner every time. Not only was I seeing the mountain's beauty and doing something that few people living in the area do, I was challenging myself and surprising myself by accomplishing more than I thought I could.

After this I looked at my fears and insecurities and wondered about which challenge I would like to tackle next. The next challenge I undertook was acting in a play. I had been a professor for a few years and found it enjoyable. Acting in a play seemed a whole lot scarier. In the next two years, I acted in two plays and enjoyed them a great deal. Once again, I surprised myself by doing something that I thought was impossible for me.

We must believe in ourselves. Before the hiking trip on Easter weekend, my belief in myself was limited. I believed I could only do the easy things in life. However, completing that hike taught me that I could also do difficult things in life. Riding up the mountain and acting in the plays verified that idea.

I also saw that not only had my belief in myself changed, but belief itself had also changed, to certainty. I went from believing I could only do the easy things to believing that I could also do the difficult things and then to knowing with certainty that I could accomplish almost anything I set out to do. Writing this book has been my latest challenge, and I approached it without any doubt of accomplishing it.

The other lesson in all of this is that belief in ourselves carries over to other aspects of our lives. If we have a poor belief about ourselves, then we will have poor self-confidence and self-esteem, and it will affect other areas of life. However, if we have a strong belief in ourselves, then we will have strong self-confidence, which will spill over into all aspects of life.

Belief in ourselves, or self-confidence, is critical to living life successfully. I see many people with so much inside but who are afraid to try anything because they lack the self-confidence. I want to really encourage everyone to try new things, to challenge yourself and go into the challenge believing you can do it. Just watch what happens.

Personal Growth Exercise:

Make a list of challenges that you would like to undertake. Start by simply writing down every idea you think of without evaluating it. Once you're finished, look the list over and evaluate them, then determine timelines for undertaking them. For example, pick one that you would like to do this coming month, pick a few for the next year, others for the next five years, and leave some as long term with no set time to tackle them.

Once you're ready to undertake a challenge, turn it into a written goal and focus on it. It will happen!

Stop and complete this written exercise before going on!

Be part of the successful 2 percent and complete the exercise now!

Summary

Belief in self is critical to success in any area of life. We need to evaluate how strong or weak our self-confidence is at a particular moment. Then we need to work toward improving our self-confidence by finding challenges and then completing them successfully. This will raise our self-image and make future challenges easier to achieve.

It is one thing to hope or believe that we can achieve something, it is much better to be certain that we can do it. We need to raise the level of belief in ourselves to certainty. Just think how easy something would be if we were certain that we could do it before we even started.

Once we have improved our self-confidence, we can start to challenge ourselves in different areas. We can try new things that we might have found to be intimidating before. I find it unbelievable what I can achieve today compared to before I started my personal growth.

Chapter 12: Yes You Can!

*You Will Never Know How Much
You Can Change Yourself*

Action is Critical

One of the difficulties about writing a self-help book is not being sure what you, the reader, will get out of it. The reason I put exercises in the book is so you'll *do* activities and learn the lessons better. That will make the book's points more meaningful. I firmly believe that only by action can you achieve your goals and succeed.

I learned this in high school chemistry. One day our teacher told us that sodium was very reactive with water. Those of us who were listening heard this fact and some even wrote it down, but no one knew what it really meant. About a month later during chemistry laboratory, the teacher took a small piece of sodium and placed it in a petri dish. Then he put some water on it. At first we weren't that interested since we had all seen something get wet before. However, we were astonished when instead of getting wet, the sodium burst into flames in a very violent reaction. It was completely consumed within a matter of seconds. Seeing that reaction was critical to understanding what the teacher meant.

Just as we needed to see that reaction to understand the teacher's lesson, only by doing can you accomplish. You can read a million self-help and motivational books, but they won't benefit you one bit unless you do what the authors recommend. You will never know how much you can change until you have *done* something yourself.

You Can Achieve Almost Anything

I have found this chapter the hardest to write because it is the least definite. The previous chapters were about things that I have experienced and lived personally, but this chapter is about the limitless possibilities that exist in your life and not what I have experienced in my life. You truly have no limits except those you put on yourself.

When I say, "*you will never know how much you can change yourself*", I mean that no matter what you achieve in life, there will always be the possibility of achieving more. I'm not suggesting that you should always be chasing more, but possibilities are always there if you want them. We usually accomplish less in life than we could because we limit ourselves. We become our own worst enemy.

Many people I know think of winning the lottery or retirement as the end. I hear things like, "I'm going to play golf every day," or "I'm going to go fishing every day." These people don't do well in retirement or after winning the lottery. If their only reason to get out of bed in the morning is to do the same thing that they've done for the past year, they'll end up staying in bed. People need to have a purpose in life or they'll become unhappy and unmotivated to do anything.

If you won $10 million in the lottery, what would you do? It's nice to dream, but reality is usually much different. Personally, I think winning the lottery would be a great burden. Life would become focused on the money—how to protect it, how to minimize income taxes, how to invest it, how to spend it, and so on. I know when we think of that prize now, it sounds great. However, after the euphoria wears off and reality sets in, life would be different in many ways, some good and some bad.

I don't buy lottery tickets because I'm afraid that I might win and that would change my life. If I did win $10 million, I think

I would find 10 friends, churches, and charitable organizations and give each one $1 million.

But let's return to the question. If you won $10 million, what would you do? Let's look down the road five years. What do you do each day? How do you spend your time? Is your life full of meaning? If it is, you are unusual. Almost every story I have read about people who won a lottery was a story of a ruined life. Often their lives were so empty after they won that they turned to drugs and alcohol.

It doesn't matter where you are in life today; you can change yourself in the present moment (remember that the present is the only time in which you have that power) so that your future is better. If you do this every day, then every following day will be better. You don't need to progress with giant steps. Baby steps work just fine. But the key is consistent improvement.

When I was studying to become an accountant and my classmates completed their exams after three long hard years of work and study, many fell into the trap of letdown. They had worked hard and been so focused on this great goal that they failed to set a subsequent goal. Since they didn't have another goal to strive toward, some fell into the trap of just doing what was in their lives. For an accountant, there is always an endless amount of work, so they ended up working a lot of extra time and not creating new goals. Since I had teaching as my long-term goal, becoming an accountant was just a milestone along the way. My friend Dave wanted to be a lawyer, so this was just a milestone along the path he had chosen. But those who had no subsequent goal often got lost in their work.

Individuals who achieve great things or have very successful lives have goals like we set earlier for five years, ten years, and twenty years ahead. They frequently update them so that when they accomplish one goal, they have the next to strive toward. Next goals don't have to be a continuation of previous goals. They might be in a different area of life, such as a relationship goal, a health goal, or a personal growth goal.

It is not unusual for people to progress through education goals, then career goals, relationship goals, family goals, and so on.

No matter what your focus is, you should always have some career goals because in today's world, if you're not growing in your career, you'll be falling behind. Even when relationship and family goals become a bigger part of your life, you need to maintain career goals such as learning new software, taking a course to enhance your skills, or learning whatever is appropriate for your career.

By always having future goals planned out, you will always be focused on where you are going. You are guaranteed to get a lot further in life if you know where it is you're headed.

Know Your Big Picture

> *You must find a cause to believe in or spend the rest of your lives compensating yourself for failure*
> John Powell

It always amused me that when I counseled students and asked them what the big picture of their lives was, many either didn't know or hadn't thought about it. The only goal they possessed was finishing the degree that they were currently undertaking. There was a giant void after that.

I encouraged them to start thinking of the big picture of their lives. It is not a specific goal or set of goals but simply what they saw for their life in general terms. My big picture was to be a teacher. I didn't know the details beyond that image.

I was successful in my career because I was fortunate to have had good direction early in life. However, it wasn't until my twenties that I figured things out. A career in accounting suited my gifts well. A career in teaching meant discovering and developing more gifts and talents that I was blessed with.

I am happy with my life and feel successful because I did and still am doing what I was designed to do.

No matter what your age, you should have a big picture for the remainder of your life. If your big picture is what you currently have, then you have stopped growing and have started dying - not a happy idea.

In order to clarify and develop your big picture, let's do an exercise. If you are twenty or thirty years old, this exercise will be much different than if you are sixty or seventy years old. A big picture of a future of fifty or sixty years is much different than the big picture of preparing your bucket list. However, a big picture is critical at any age.

Personal Growth Exercise:

Describe the big picture that you currently see for your life. Try to include as many areas of your life as possible and don't just focus on your career. What do you see happening in the areas of family, relationships, health, career, finances, hobbies, challenges? Remember that this is not a lot of specific goals as much as a general, broad description of what you want or expect for your future.

If you are having trouble seeing your big picture, then try this exercise instead. List one hundred things that you want to do before you die. Whether you're twenty or eighty, you can make this list by simply writing down (without evaluation or judgment of any kind) things that you would like to do assuming you're able to do them.

You may find it difficult to complete a list of one hundred items. Keep going because once you run out of ideas, you will probably start getting to the really good ones that you haven't let yourself dream about but that may be your real big picture.

Stop and complete this written exercise before going on!

Be part of the successful 2 percent and complete the exercise now!

Decide What You Must Give

The more clearly you've described your big picture and set goals to match it, the easier it will be for you to see what you'll need to give to get what you want. I had to give years of studying, earning degrees, and working in accounting offices to become skilled enough to be an accounting professor. I never stopped studying, and I later became a professor in computing as well.

If you want to be a doctor, you'll need to study and practice medicine until you're a skilled physician. But the giving won't stop then, as you'll have to continue to learn to keep abreast of the advances in medicine.

For example look at Mark, who wanted to be a mechanic. He chose to study and spend time working on his trade to be a skilled mechanic. While many of his workmates stopped learning, he continued to take classes and soon rose above the others to become an outstanding mechanic. Mark gave what was required to rise above the rest.

To achieve anything, you'll need to give something of yourself. You'll have to learn skills and then continue to keep them up. The more successful you want to be, the more effort you will have to give to rise to the top and to stay at the top once you've arrived. There are no free rides in life. As Zig Ziglar says, "*The elevator to success is closed but the stairs are always open.*"

The only jobs that you can get in life without giving of yourself are not jobs you would dream of having for a career. I call these "motivational jobs" because they motivate you to get a better job. The same is true with anything in life: the things that come with little effort on your part are not usually what you want.

If you have set goals and are determined to achieve them, then you see the effort, or cost, as nothing compared to the benefit that you are going to receive. It is simply the cost-benefit analysis: you weigh the cost against the value of the benefit to see if something is worth pursuing.

However, if your goals are unclear or if you're not focused on them, then you might focus too much on the cost and be unwilling to pay the price. For example, if you are dedicated to being a doctor, then the years of preparation are a price that you are willing to pay. But if you are not *dedicated* to becoming a doctor and instead focus on the years of study and preparation as undesirable, then you will probably not be willing to pay the price to be a doctor.

I know I was so dedicated to being a professor that I never looked at the study as a cost or hardship but as a pleasure. I truly enjoyed my years of schooling and working in accounting firms as I got ready to teach. If you don't enjoy the time of preparation, then there is a strong possibility that you won't enjoy what you're seeking.

I saw a student who got straight A's in his classes and earned his accounting degree. When he became an accountant, he hated the work and quit after less than a year. When I asked him why, he said that he never enjoyed the study to get his degree. He had just done it because his father was an accountant. He was trying to please his father rather than living his own dreams.

When you learn a new skill for a hobby, you don't think of that work as undesirable but as part of the pleasure of the hobby. Striving toward any goal works the same way. The preparation is part of the process, and it should be as enjoyable as the goal that you have set for yourself.

You can learn more about paying the price for goals in the book, *What Price Are You Willing to Pay?* by John C. Maxwell. I feel that he presents the whole subject excellently.

Although I use terms like "cost" and "effort" when describing preparation, it really is nothing more than enjoying every part of what you have chosen to do. Remember, your attitude is everything in life. It will determine how you see things before you do them and also how you view them after they are completed.

Attitude of Gratitude

To Thine Own Self Be True.
Polonius in Shakespeare's *Hamlet*

If you want to have the greatest success in any area of your life or you want to experience life with the greatest degree of fulfillment, then adopting an *"Attitude of Gratitude"* is important.

I discovered this when I was just beginning therapy after getting divorced. I was bitter and angry because I felt that I had lost so much in the divorce. My therapist gave me a homework exercise to list the ten good things that I got from the marriage. I told him that I could easily give him a list of the ten things that I lost in the divorce but that he was crazy to think that I had gotten anything good out of it.

He told me that every situation has two sides. We need to look at the good side and the bad side in order to better understand what really happened. Once we've done that, we must forget the bad things and focus on the good things so that we can find peace. Focusing on the bad things will only lead to hurt, resentment, and anger, which in turn will lead to more problems in the future.

I went home from that session sure that I couldn't do the exercise, but since I trusted my therapist, I was determined to do the best I could do. At first I really struggled with the exercise. However, by the time the next meeting had arrived, I was a different person. Not only had I made a list of the ten things that I had gotten out of the marriage, but I had also realized that the things that I had received were of infinite value to me and the things that I had given up were insignificant. I don't mean valuable in terms of money but in terms of my set of values. After that, instead of being bitter and angry at what I had lost, I was happy and thankful for what I had gained.

This exercise is an incredible one. We can use it whenever we're struggling with a situation. First, we can list the bad parts of the situation. This should be easy since we're usually already focused on them. (By the way, there is healing power in writing down the negatives and then later filing or throwing them away). Second, we can make a list of the good parts of the situation. Then we can forget the bad parts and focus on the good parts. This is truly an excellent way to get over a bad situation and find peace.

I know that it may look like there is nothing good about your situation. I have found that every situation has both positive and negative features. If you focus on the bad, it may break you. *If you focus on the good, it will grow you.* Adversity is a part of everyone's life. *It is not the adversity that determines who you are but your response to it.*

As an example, let's look at two people with similar skills who get laid off. One is bitter and angry and feels wronged by the layoff. He then starts feeling sorry for himself (which is very dangerous) because of what happened *to* him. This carries over into his job search, making it more difficult for him to get another job. By feeling sorry for himself, he may also turn to drugs and alcohol to numb his bad feelings. He has started to self-destruct.

The other individual is angry for a short time but then sees that this is an opportunity to get a new job. Maybe a job with a better company or a better boss! She is excited by the opportunity and goes out and enthusiastically pursues another job. She probably will get a better job and is unlikely to turn to drugs and alcohol because she doesn't need to numb her feelings.

Both people faced the same situation, but each had a very different response to it and a different outcome. Many people who run their own businesses started after getting laid off from a job. These people are often happier than they were in their jobs and look back at getting laid off with gratitude. They wouldn't be where they are today without having been forced to evaluate their lives and what they wanted to do.

In everything that you do in life, you need to adopt an *Attitude of Gratitude* and view every situation as a positive growing experience. One way I use my *Attitude of Gratitude* is by saying grace before every meal. No matter where I am or who I'm with, I always stop before I eat and thank God for whatever is good in my life at that time. You can always find something good in your life if you just look for it.

An important part of adopting a positive attitude is resolving past hurts - we all have them. We do this through forgiveness. If we feel that someone has wronged us, we live with negative feelings that if left unchecked, can lead to serious problems. However, if we can forgive that other person, we can get past these feelings. We will feel like a huge burden has been removed from our bodies.

Forgiveness is something that you do for you, not for the other person. After all, a person who wronged you may never know how you feel and may be unable to receive your forgiveness. If you focus on yourself, forgiveness is easier. It is freeing. One approach to forgiveness is to think about the other person and realize that he or she acted out of inner pain. If you can't forgive, then you carry those feelings around through life like dragging an anchor behind you. But if you can forgive the person, you can move on with your life.

I'm not suggesting that forgiveness is easy, but it is very important for you to resolve these past issues. I know of no other way of changing from living in the past to living in the present and working toward your goals for the future. It is difficult to develop an *Attitude of Gratitude* if you haven't forgiven people in your past.

My friends have a little boy named Derek who I feel is a model for what it means to have an *Attitude of Gratitude*. One evening at dinner, Derek's mother asked him to say grace as he often did. The whole family bowed their heads, but there was complete silence. Finally, a little voice said, "God, I don't like what we have for dinner tonight, but I want to thank you anyway."

That is the true *Attitude of Gratitude*. In every situation in life, whether in good or bad circumstances, you need to look for something to be thankful for. It will change how you experience your life, and you will be much happier because of it. You will also influence the people around you with your attitude, so you need to focus on having a wonderful attitude.

This *Attitude of Gratitude* can really change your life. Many people tend to focus on the negative more than the positive. When you talk with people, some only tell you what is wrong with their lives or the weather. These are seldom uplifting encounters. However, if you choose to share the good and ask others what's going well in their lives, then the focus switches and you'll have an uplifting exchange. The other person will walk away feeling a little better about their day also.

Ask yourself, what's good in your life today?

- ☑ Can you see?
- ☑ Can you hear?

- ☑ Can you walk?
- ☑ Do you live in a free country?
- ☑ Are you able to choose what you do today?
- ☑ Is there someone in your life who loves you?
- ☑ Is the weather nice?

All of these are good things that not everyone can enjoy. For each of these items that you possess, you have reason to be thankful.

Summary

Action is critical to anything you want to accomplish in life. You can't just think it or wish for it or read about it, you must do. The more that you do, the more you can do. Just like your physical muscles, your life will grow larger as you accomplish more. The more you give of yourself, the more results you will see.

Once you examine situations in your life, it is easy to come up with two lists, a list of bad things and a list of good things. You should forget the bad things and focus on the good things all day. You will find that the list will grow longer every day.

Forgiveness plays an important part in your getting over your past and living in the present. No matter what the situation, forgive and forget, and move on with life. It is easier said than done but it is critical for your freedom.

In everything that you do, you should adopt an *Attitude of Gratitude* and fill your life with diamonds.

Chapter 13: Let's Go!

The best time to get started is right now!

I hope that you have enjoyed reading *Attitude Determines Destiny*. If you're excited to use this material but are unsure of where to start, this chapter will help.

I want to introduce a program I call GAS, which will energize your life in a short period of time. I believe that if you follow this program, you will see amazing changes within the next thirty days.

GAS is an acronym for:

GOALS + *ACTION* = SUCCESS

Here is a thirty-day challenge that will demonstrate the power of goals.

Step 1 Set a Goal

Pick one of your goals. The goal should not be too big but one that you really want to accomplish.

Write the goal on a three-by-five card and carry it with you for the next thirty days. Refer to it several times every day. Read it aloud as often as possible.

Write your goal on a piece of paper and make at least five copies and hang them up in your home, your car, and your work space so that you'll be reminded of your goal often. Think about the goal every time you see one of your signs.

Review your goal the first thing every morning and the last thing every night.

These reminders will establish your goal firmly in your conscious and subconscious minds. This will also help you focus on your goal.

Step 2 Take Action

No goal is any good without *action*! To succeed, you must take action to move toward your goal. To do this, you need two things:

1) Focus. You must be truly focused on just one goal for the next thirty days. You must think about it often. When you work toward it, you must do so with definite purpose. You must really want to accomplish it.
2) Time. You must spend at least one hour *every* day working toward your goal. You must do this *every day*, and you must truly dedicate that hour to achieving your goal. Remember seven hours one day a week does not equal one hour seven days a week. The consistency is critical.

Step 3 Achieve Success

If you have diligently followed the program for all thirty days, you will probably be amazed at the results. You may have achieved your goal before the thirty days were up. Whenever you have completed your goal, pick another goal and repeat the process. If you start with small goals and work up to bigger goals, then you will be increasing your confidence over time.

If you did not achieve your goal, determine why. Did you use the program properly? Did you pick a goal that was too big or a goal that was too difficult to do in thirty days? Once you have determined the reason, make the necessary changes and then do this exercise again for the next thirty days and see what happens.

I believe that this exercise is truly powerful. By focusing on just one goal and taking action toward it, you can accomplish it and then move to the next one. You must work toward goals like climbing a flight of stairs: by taking one step at a time.

It is also very enlightening to see how much you can achieve in such a short time.

The sky is the limit. If you do the exercises and put the challenge in this chapter into practice, then you should have a good beginning for a successful future.

Have a wonderful life!

P.S. I would like to hear from you and know how this book helped you. You can contact me on Facebook or LinkedIn or at www.BruceRaine.com or at:

Bruce Raine
c/o Arbutus TLC, Inc.
1004 Commercial Ave # 1095
Anacortes, WA 98221

Appendix A: The Three Pillars of a Successful Life

There are three pillars that support a successful life. We must choose to develop these continually. We are never finished with any of the three, and we'll use them simultaneously throughout our lives.

Pillar 1 ADD

ADD stands for *"Attitude Determines Destiny."* Our attitude in life will determine how successful we will be. The best possible attitude is an *Attitude of Gratitude*.

Pillar 2 GLUE

GLUE stands for "God Loves Us Eternally." I believe that the most important part of a successful life is a relationship with God that puts him first and foremost in our lives. This relationship provides us with values, guidance, and wisdom. It leads to success in all areas of life.

Pillar 3 GAS

GAS stands for "Goals + *Action* = Success."

By using this process, we can achieve amazing results in a short period of time.

Appendix B: The Only Laws We Need

I believe that there are too many laws today. We would be better served by using just the Ten Commandments. If everyone followed them, there would be no crime, no wars, no family conflicts, etc. It would be easy to know what was right and wrong in any situation. Below are the Ten Commandments that I adapted from the book of Deuteronomy in the Bible and personalized:

\# 1 I shall have no other gods before God.

\# 2 I shall not make for myself any idol.

\# 3 I shall not take the name of the Lord in vain.

\# 4 I shall observe the Sabbath day and keep it holy.

\# 5 I shall honor my father and my mother.

\# 6 I shall not murder.

\# 7 I shall not commit adultery.

\# 8 I shall not steal.

\# 9 I shall not lie.

\# 10 I shall not covet.

Appendix C: 100% Money Back GUARANTEE!

I want to GUARANTEE that this book is worth the purchase price or I will give you your money back – 100% of your purchase price.

If you read this book and do the exercises in the book and feel that it is not worth the price that you paid, I will give you your money back.

It is extremely important to me that you are satisfied with the book. If you would like to send me a letter telling about how you liked or disliked the book, I would truly appreciate it.

However, if you are so dissatisfied that you want your money back, just complete the steps below:

1. Send me a letter verifying that you read the whole book.
2. Send me copies of all the written exercises verifying that you did them. You must do the exercises to get the maximum benefit from the book.
3. Send me a letter explaining why you are dissatisfied. I would like to know how you feel this book let you down.
4. Return the book regardless of the condition.
5. Send me a copy of the receipt showing the date and amount of the purchase.

About the Author

Bruce Raine is a motivational speaker and author living in Anacortes, Washington. He was born in Halifax, Nova Scotia, Canada. He moved to the San Francisco Bay Area and was a professor of accounting and computing at California State University in Hayward.

Personal growth has been a passion of his for the past thirty years and continues every day. With God at the center of his life and his passion for personal growth, he has achieved a level of contentment and peace in his life that he never dreamed possible.

This book was written to help people who are going through problems similar to those he encountered. He spent his childhood in the home of an alcoholic and his adulthood in a series of unsuccessful relationships. With God's love and through counseling and personal growth he was able to deal with these past problems and find peace.

Bruce welcomes your comments and suggestions.

He also conducts seminars and workshops based upon the ideas in this book. Go to www.BruceRaine.com

Made in the USA
Charleston, SC
24 June 2012